The Freedom Paradox

THE FREEDOM PARADOX

Is Unbridled Freedom Dividing America?

BOBBY ALBERT

NEW YORK

LONDON • NASHVILLE • MELBOURNE • VANCOUVER

THE FREEDOM PARADOX

Is Unbridled Freedom Dividing America?

Published in New York, New York, by Morgan James Publishing. Morgan James is a trademark of Morgan James, LLC. www.MorganJamesPublishing.com

ISBN 9781642796445 paperback
ISBN 9781642796452 eBook
Library of Congress Control Number: 2019943987

Cover Design by:
Ryan Biore

Interior Design by:
Chris Treccani
www.3dogcreative.net

Morgan James is a proud partner of Habitat for Humanity Peninsula and Greater Williamsburg. Partners in building since 2006.

Get involved today! Visit
MorganJamesPublishing.com/giving-back

To my wife, Susan, whose support and friendship I have enjoyed for forty-six years and counting, and to our three sons, Rob, Brian, and Kyle, who are my life's legacy and of whom I'm very proud.

TABLE OF CONTENTS

PART ONE:

Freedom *and* Responsibility

CHAPTER ONE:

America, Who Are You?

Something Has Changed about Our Great Nation

America will never be destroyed from the outside.
If we falter and lose our freedoms, it will be because we
destroyed ourselves.
—Abraham Lincoln

America, who are you? You have changed so much in recent years that I no longer recognize you.

The leaders of our country said to expect change, and change has indeed been occurring at warp speed. However, change is not always good. I personally enjoy change, but I do not like unpleasant surprises. And in recent years, I have been surprised often, though not in a good way.

While many of the changes to our nation have been necessary and good, may I suggest that we have also changed a few things that should not have been changed? The foundational core values and purpose of our nation should never change, yet they have been subtly shifting for generations.

As a result, our nation is at a tipping point, much like the story of the boiling frog. As the story goes, if a frog is placed in boiling water, it will jump out. But if it is placed in cool and pleasant water that

3

is gradually heated, it will not perceive the danger until it is too late and will be cooked to death.

The same principle applies to people. Those who are unable or unwilling to react to significant changes that occur *gradually* will eventually suffer undesirable consequences.

The American people sense that the "water" of our great nation is no longer cool and pleasant. That is why more and more people in America are thinking, *Something is not right. I feel like a stranger in my own country.*

This sentiment is reflected in a June 2019 Gallup poll, revealing that 66 percent of Americans are "dissatisfied with the way things are going in the United States at this time." Only 32 percent of those polled were satisfied.[1]

As I wonder about the legacy we will leave for our children and grandchildren, I am concerned we are drifting into an uncertain and dangerous future.

Reflect to Connect

1. Do you recognize America today compared to when you were a child?
2. How do you feel today about the direction of America compared to when you were a child?

According to these statistics, we seem to be trudging through a deep valley of despair instead of enjoying the fruited plain of blessing described in "America the Beautiful." How did we get to this point? I believe we find the root cause of the problem in what I call the Life and Liberty Equation:

Freedom + Responsibility = Life, Liberty, and the Pursuit of Happiness

You see, America was established on the core values of freedom *and* responsibility. When founded, our country had a healthy tension between personal responsibilities and the vast freedoms that we enjoy. However, we have lost that healthy tension.

The problem is on the left side of the equation: we no longer think, speak, and behave responsibly in our culture, and that, in turn, has created many of the detrimental changes that have occurred in our great nation.

When our focus and motivation are based only on "my rights" (freedoms) and we neglect our corresponding responsibilities, chaos ensues.

When our thinking revolves around our personal rights and freedoms alone, our attitude and behaviors become all about *me*—a self-centeredness rooted in pride. We have all heard that "pride comes before the fall." That "fall" could be the downfall of "We the People of the United States."

Conversely, when our focus and motivation are based on both our personal freedoms *and* our responsibilities, our attitude and behaviors become all about *we*—an ability to make decisions for the common good.

You are sure to have observed how often we emphasize *me* or *I* today: iPhone, iPad, iGod, a ".me" URL, and other products, services, and movements whose names highlight the letters *M* and *E*. Business advertising also makes it clear that it is all about *me*.

Economists report that about two-thirds of the U.S. economy is driven by consumer spending. Our citizens have access to all the world has to offer. We're encouraged to acquire anything we desire, which intensifies our drive for self-gratification.

The American economy enables you to indulge every physical desire you have. It is easy to crave and accumulate things and obsess over your status and importance, all while neglecting any sense of responsibility. Have you considered the word *consume*? The last two letters spell *me*!

The unbridled pursuit of freedom sees everything through the perspective of *me*, while the dialogue of responsibility always includes the perspective of *we*. The warp-speed expansion of this emphasis on *me* and *I* is pushing us faster and faster toward the exclusion of *we* and the worship of *me* as an idol.

Where do you think our . . .

Divisiveness,

Disunity,

Detachment by society's elite,

Discord among the poor,

Dishonorable name-calling,

Dishonesty, and

Disrespectfulness

. . . come from?

You have heard that "a house divided against itself cannot stand." Well, when we pursue freedoms without regard to the principles of responsibility, we encounter the emptiness, frustration, and loneliness that are so evident in our divided nation today. Without that healthy tension, the Life and Liberty Equation breaks down, and we now understand why over two-thirds of Americans think the country is on the wrong track.

So, how did our sense of responsibility disappear? It is a subject we will explore in this book.

Being responsible is not about freedoms you give up; it's about freedoms you choose not to exercise.

Some might argue that binding our freedoms with responsibility will limit our freedoms. But don't miss the wisdom of **The Freedom Paradox**:

> *The more we behave irresponsibly, the more freedoms we lose. The more we embrace responsibility, the greater freedoms we enjoy.*

Individual rights assume individual responsibility. When people behave responsibly, they understand that there are behaviors and actions that are just off limits, things they just don't do, and they establish discipline not to cross those boundary lines.

Think about it: just about every sport, game board, and video game has boundary lines. When you cross over those boundary lines, you are penalized or suffer negative consequences. However, between those boundary lines, you have a lot of freedom to play the game within fair and reasonable rules.

Therefore, let us adhere to a higher standard:

> *Let us do what is responsible instead of what is permissible.*

Let's leverage our individual rights for the benefit of others to prevent our freedom from devouring itself and us.

America's Heart Condition

America, what is your heart condition? No, I'm not talking about the health of the physical condition of your heart. I'm talking about your overall well-being. The truth is, you have not "guarded your heart" and your mind. You've ignored your responsibilities as you've pursued your freedoms. And this lax approach has impacted your mind, body, and soul; your attitudes, emotions, and thoughts.

Outward success is an inside job.

In fact, America, you live this life for today, as though there is no tomorrow.

America, you may be asking, "How do I know the condition of my heart?"

First, you must understand there is a war going on inside you. Perhaps I can explain it with an illustration: It is like two dogs fighting inside you. One is a force of evil, and the other is a force of good.

Which one wins?

It is the one who is the strongest.

And the strongest dog is the one you feed the most.

If we feed and encourage our desire for freedom and neglect our corresponding responsibilities, the "beast" we have fed will one day turn and strip even our tightly gripped freedoms from our hands.

*All by ourselves, we have complete freedom to make
a judgment . . . We decide whether we tell the truth or
benefit from telling lies. We're the ones that decide: Do I
hate? Or am I filled with love? We're the ones who decide:
Will I think only about myself, or do I care for others?*
–Jimmy Carter

Reflect to Connect

1. How well do you behave when you exercise the use of your wonderful freedoms without responsibilities?
2. How well do you self-govern your responsibilities when you exercise the use of your wonderful freedoms?
3. Which "dog" do you feed the most (freedom or responsibility)? How do your actions prove your answer to this question?

If you really want to change the condition of your heart and direction, America, the time is now.

The Time to Act Is Now

The average lifespan in the United States is 78 years. That's 28,470 days. If you factor in leap years, that's about 28,500 days.

Now let's suppose you have a pad of sticky notes 28,500 high, and every one of these sticky notes represents one day of your life. And every day you peel off another sticky note and fill up that note with everything you did during the day.

But after that day is over, it's gone, and you have one fewer days. Now, you and I don't know how much time we have, but here's what we do know. We know that the amount of time that we have is limited, and every day we don't use our lives for good is a wasted day. And we don't have an unlimited supply of days.

I don't know where you are in your life journey today. You may be starting a new chapter in your life. Maybe you're entering college. Maybe you're beginning a marriage or family, or maybe you're starting a chapter described as retirement or have recently become a grandparent.

As we continue on our journey, all of us have key opportunities to live our lives for the good. When we reach certain milestones in our journey, these opportunities seem all the more important, and we feel that we are there, at that point in time, for a reason.

That is the feeling I sense now, and it is why I feel so compelled to share my observations on the cultural changes occurring in our country.

As a nation, we certainly know how to embrace and pursue freedom, but in this pursuit, we have trampled the rights and freedoms of others—neglecting the twin sister of responsibility that always accompanies lasting freedom.

The Freedom Paradox is an attempt to begin a dialogue on these important national issues, sharing what you may not *want* to hear but what we all *need* to hear. My intent is to keep my talking points non-political, even though I will refer to our country's leaders in general.

I hope you will allow our journeys to merge for a brief time. Will you join me as we explore how to live out the core values of the United States of America by embracing lives rich with freedom and guided by responsibility?

Reflect to Connect

1. How do you live each day with intention?
2. In what ways have you noticed people embracing their own freedoms, with little concern for the rights and freedoms of others?

CHAPTER TWO:

Preserve the Core

To Prosper, We Must Protect Our Core Ideology

Then join hand in hand, brave Americans all!
By uniting we stand, by dividing we fall.
—**John Dickinson, "The Liberty Song of 1768"**

America almost didn't exist. And the factors threatening her demise hold some lessons for those who seek to understand our current situation.

A revolution that was underfunded and underprepared in nearly every way should have failed to guarantee anything like a lasting nation. Despite the justice and truth of the Declaration of Independence, words could not pay bills, sign treaties, or defend borders. Early attempts at governance were shaky, at best.

The Articles of Confederation barely bound the thirteen new states together, and working together in war and peace alike proved difficult. Each state looked to its own interests, despite the harm caused to the whole.

Because the Articles required unanimous agreement between the states for any decision, soldiers in Valley Forge starved and froze. After the war, both tiny Rhode Island and wealthy New York succeeded in blocking proposed tariffs the new country desperately needed to pay the starving, ill soldiers at Newburgh, New Jersey, who deserved their pensions, and to pay installments on the millions America owed in war debt to France and Holland.

No one state was willing to accept the entire responsibility of the French debt or the payment of military pensions, and the Confederation Congress as a whole lacked the will, the organization, and the money to address these problems.

But like a hero in a fairy tale who discovers he has possessed the key to his own salvation all along, America knew the source of her latent strength. She just needed to acknowledge it.

On the same day that the United States declared its independence, it created a committee to design a seal of the United States, an emblem that other nations could recognize when making agreements with her. Thomas Jefferson, Benjamin Franklin, and John Adams all submitted designs, and they consulted a Philadelphia artist for advice. That artist, Pierre du Simitiere, drew a seal that included the motto:

E Pluribus Unum: out of many, one.

It was not a new concept. Franklin had earlier drawn and published a cartoon of the snake cut in thirteen pieces with the title "Join or Die." The United States had sent ambassadors to France and Holland as a single entity. But fears of being lost in the company of larger states plagued the smaller ones, and unwillingness to grant too much power to obstinate provincials kept the larger states from truly embracing the concept that the United States, in order to survive, must truly become one.

The various committees charged with designing the Great Seal of the United States worked on and off for six years, until 1782. Though the elements of the final design had changed over that six years, one element that remained the same was that motto: *E Pluribus Unum.*

Augustine had used it in *The City of God.* Cicero had used it to describe the natural bonds of family and friendship that formed the basis of government. A London magazine used it as a way to declare itself a kind of prototype of *Reader's Digest*. But not until the summer of 1787 did the cautious and suspicious states understand its full power.

For that summer, the summer of the Constitutional Convention, the founders of the nation brought all their doubts and fears and suspicions into the open, along with all of their hopes and ambitions for the new country.

They spoke under a veil of secrecy that allowed them the privilege of honesty and plain dealing. They grappled with the reality that none of them were going to get anything ideal. But they could come together and make a nation that could work.

Men as different as Democrat Madison and Federalist Hamilton could set their differences aside and agree on principles. Small states like Massachusetts could come to terms with large states like Virginia.

America exists because of those leaders, because they could look at the Great Seal they had adopted and affirm its central truth. We are all different. We all want the best for ourselves. But when we come together in agreement, no one part taking advantage of another but each pulling its own weight according to its own abilities, we are powerful.[2]

Our unity is the key to our liberty.

Once these leaders believed in our need for unity—out of many, one—they had the faith and courage to act upon that belief to bring about the birth of the Constitution of the United States.

This is why the seal of the United States meant so much to the founders of our great nation. This is why a sense of excitement, enthusiasm, and passion stirs within each of us when we:

- Sing or listen to our national anthem, "The Star-Spangled Banner," written during the War of 1812 by Francis Scott Key. The song was inspired by what he witnessed as the British attacked Fort McHenry. After the fort withstood the day-long assault, and as a new day dawned, he could see the American flag still flying.

- See the American flag unfurled by the wind. Its stripes represent the unity of the original Thirteen Colonies, and its stars represent the unity of the fifty states. Red symbolizes hardiness and valor; white symbolizes purity and innocence; and blue represents vigilance, perseverance, and justice.
- See the Statue of Liberty as a universal symbol of freedom from tyranny and oppression—the torch in her uplifted right hand lighting the way to liberty and the tablet cradled in her left arm memorializing the date of the Declaration of Independence, JULY IV MDCCLXXVI (July 4, 1776).
- See the bald eagle, with its fierce beauty and proud independence, chosen appropriately by our Founding Fathers as the emblem of our nation, symbolizing the strength and freedoms of America.

Reflect to Connect

1. What do you think and feel when you hear or sing our national anthem?
2. How does the common belief in American ideas serve to unite even diverse groups of Americans?
3. Will you contemplate the power of our common beliefs the next time you stand in a crowd to recite the national anthem?

This is why we, as Americans, have the faith and courage to act upon our belief that each of us can accomplish the "American Dream":

- Get a good education
- Work hard
- Buy a house

- Achieve prosperity and success

This is why America is truly known as the "land of opportunity," where we can achieve anything we put our mind to, no matter who we are.

This is why military members put themselves in harm's way every day in enemy territory to protect our sovereign nation; they believe strongly in freedom from tyranny and oppression.

For example, consider those soldiers who proudly landed on the shores of Normandy, France, on D-Day, June 6, 1944, which was the beginning of the end of the WWII. The men who fought in that invasion forever changed the course of nations and altered people's perception of courage in the face of overwhelming odds.

This is why our nation is known for American Exceptionalism. Even five decades after America gained independence, French political analyst Alexis de Tocqueville remarked on the exceptional character of the United States: America has a history that is inherently different from those of other nations. Other nations are defined by ethnicity, geography, common heritage, social class, or hierarchal structures. But America has a special character uniquely marked by a distinct set of ideas, bonded together by a shared commitment to the democratic principles of liberty, equality, individualism, and *laissez faire* economics.

Tis the business of little minds to shrink; but he whose heart is firm, and whose conscience approves his conduct, will pursue his principles unto death.
–Thomas Paine

One thing I have come to understand is that you cannot buy these beliefs that are so deeply rooted inside America, and this is why, through effective leadership, these beliefs must be regularly communicated, understood by all Americans, and lived—especially by our national leaders.

*You can buy someone's time, you can buy someone's
physical presence at a given place, you can even buy
a measured number of skilled muscular motions per hour
or day. But, you cannot buy enthusiasm; you cannot buy
initiative; you cannot buy loyalty; you cannot buy devotion
of hearts, minds, and souls.
You have to earn these things.*
–Clarence Francis

Reflect to Connect

1. Do you know someone who served in our military or sacrificed their life for our country?
2. What did they believe about America?

The Key to Extraordinary Growth

What is true about America is also true in business. Research has shown time and time again that when leaders and employees agree on a shared core ideology, this ideology provides a central core around which the "many become one," and they have even greater faith and courage to put it into practice.

For example, in the book *Built to Last*, Jim Collins and Jerry Porras looked at some of the United States' most successful corporations, many of which date back to the 1800s. Using decades of data and exacting criteria for evaluation, Collins and Porras compared three distinct groups of organizations:

- **Visionary companies**: the best of the best, described as "premier institutions in their industries, widely admired by their peers and having a long track record of making a significant impact on the world around them."

- **Comparison companies**: close competitors to the visionary companies who have achieved a high level of success but not to the extent of the visionary companies.
- **Average companies:** average-performance companies in the general stock market.

What is amazing is the extraordinary long-term financial performance of these enduring, great, visionary companies. Collins and Porras contrasted the three types of companies by showing what one dollar invested on January 1, 1926, would have grown to by December 31, 1990. Here's what they found:

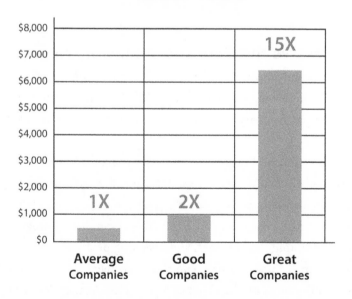

Growth of $1 Invested
1926-1990

From 1926 to 1990, your investment in the good "comparison" companies would have earned two times more than the general stock market, which isn't bad. But your investment in the great "visionary" companies would have been *fifteen times greater* than the general stock market.

Wow! So, what makes these visionary companies different? For that matter, why do only a few companies have extraordinary profits while the rest never make it to this top level? What do these super-successful companies know that the rest of us do not?

I asked myself these questions when I was trying to grow our business. And the answers I found should bring hope to *any* struggling organization—or nation.

Shocking Fact: Visionary companies are generally more ideologically driven and less purely profit driven. The same principle applies to nations. The greatest nations focus on and embrace their core ideology.

Preserve the Core and Stimulate Progress

Collins and Porras discovered that the enduring, great visionary companies did a couple of things very well. The authors summed it up by stating that visionary companies "preserved the core and stimulated progress."

These companies' core ideology was so strong that they were known to have a cult-like culture. This meant the organization's core ideology—which they define as core values plus purpose—was always fanatically protected and never changed, while they "stimulated progress" by endlessly adapting their business and operating practices.

Over time, these visionary companies changed almost everything: policies, procedures, product lines, competencies, organization structure, reward systems, strategies, tactics, and performance goals. But the *one thing* they did not change was their core ideology.

*Cult-like cultures, which preserve the core,
must be counterweighted with a huge dose of
stimulating progress.*
–Jim Collins and Jerry Porras

The Albert Companies

As a CEO of my own business for over forty years, I have seen the power of this principle with my own eyes.

At my company, we were definitely not perfect, but over time, we got more intentional about creating a great and enduring company. I introduced our company's purpose in the fall of 1996, and our company's core values in the fall of 2005.

Once I was able to articulate our core ideology—which our employees already believed and demonstrated, by the way—we were able to unite around this changeless common core, and our business took off like a rocket ship. We truly built a culture where people thrived and profits soared.

From 2005 through 2011 (the year I sold our company to a publicly traded company), we saw the following results during some of the toughest economic times:

- Revenue grew about five times (500 percent).
- Profit increased slightly more than five times (500 percent).
- We were awarded the 100 Best Companies to Work For in Texas distinction in 2011 and 2012.

Our company experienced significant growth during a time when many other companies were declining due to the Great Recession.

I believe that any leader can create a top-performing organization, and that includes those who lead national, state, and local government entities. The key is to focus on the two areas Collins and Porras identified: *preserving the core and stimulating progress.*

When we the American people commit to authentically living our changeless core values (*who* we are) and our purpose (*why* we exist), we will be able to navigate the choppy and changing waters of American life with clarity and confidence.

> *People can't live with change*
> *without a changeless core.*
> –Stephen Covey

When we believe in our core ideas, we are able to self-regulate our behaviors without all of the laws, rules and regulations, policies and procedures, and forms and documents designed by our government to micromanage our behaviors and our lives.

Reflect to Connect

1. Do you believe in the American core ideas?
2. What would you say America's core values and purpose are?
3. Do you know who you are—bone deep? What are your personal core values and life purpose? Do they align with America's?

In his book *How the Mighty Fall,* Jim Collins researched how a few of the great companies fell from their lofty positions of success. He found that in their success they became arrogant and undisciplined to pursue "more" because these companies thought they could do anything.

These companies ignored internal warning signs, and in their decline, they searched for a quick fix and took untested, bold steps. They even brought in leadership from outside the company with core values *not* aligned with theirs—further accelerating their fall.

Similar to companies, great nations can and do fall. When Rome and Greece (the birthplace of democracy) fell, they had already shifted from their core ideas.

America became a great nation by focusing on the two areas Collins and Porras identified: preserve the core and stimulate progress.

For the past several generations, as a nation, we the American people have been stimulating progress (some changes have been good, while others were not so good), but we have *not* been preserving the core. So, in the next two chapters, let's take a deeper look at both parts of our changeless core: our *core values* and our *purpose.*

core values ®

CHAPTER THREE

America's Core Values: Freedom *and* Responsibility

Guidelines for Thought, Speech, and Action

> *Liberty means responsibility.*
> *That is why most men dread it.*
> **—George Bernard Shaw**

At the end of the American Revolution, as mentioned in the previous chapter, the Continental Congress faced growing financial woes. Many disgruntled revolutionary soldiers didn't think they were going to be paid. They began contemplating whether this new country would be better off with a monarchy.

One account, as recorded by historian Robert F. Haggard, states that "a letter was handed to Washington containing the demand of some for a monarchy, and himself the king."[3] Think about that for a minute. Imagine referring to Washington not as the first president but rather as the first king of the United States: "King George I of the United States."

Washington had no such aspirations. After the signing of the Treaty of Paris in 1783, General George Washington resigned as commander-in-chief of the Continental Army and retired to his home at Mount Vernon.

Why would an individual turn down that sort of power? Washington chose to behave *responsibly*. During the war, Congress had granted significant power to Washington. Preferring the greater good of America, Washington chose not to exercise his freedom nor seize the opportunities afforded by his powerful position as a victorious commander.

I hope I shall always possess firmness and virtue enough to maintain (what I consider the most enviable of all titles) the character of an honest man.
–George Washington to Alexander Hamilton, August 28, 1788

The dangers of monarchial tyranny weren't lost on Washington, considering he and the troops had just won a battle for freedom from an oppressive monarchy, and he was not about to return this new country into the hands of such a system.

Is life so dear or peace so sweet as to be purchased at the price of chains and slavery? Forbid it, Almighty God! I know not what course others may take; but as for me, give me liberty or give me death!
–Patrick Henry

As America's first commander-in-chief, Washington's decision to resign, in essence, had much to do with two distinctive traits: character and virtue.

Washington, as did many of the other founders, understood that liberty comes from more than just laws and regulations. It comes from virtuous citizens.

Specifically, freedom thrives when citizens' character is influenced by virtue. Combined, these traits provide the self-restraint that counterbalances the social risks of giving people liberty.

The people will have virtue and intelligence to select men of virtue and wisdom. Is there no virtue among us? If there be not, we are in a wretched situation. No theoretical checks–no form of government can render us secure.
–James Madison

Are you ready to create a frame of reference—a set of criteria and guidelines—that will clearly show Americans *how* we can responsibly think and conduct ourselves?

The question above reveals the desires of almost every American I've encountered. After answering that question with a hearty yes, we then ask, "But how?"

It starts by knowing, bone deep, who we are as a nation.

Based on years of study and my own experience in leadership, I can share with you that the answer is to identify our authentic core values, regularly communicate them to the American people, and instill them into the very fabric of our nation.

The benefits to this approach are numerous, not the least of which is having clear, shared guidelines for our thinking, speech, and actions.

It's not hard to make decisions when you know what your values are.
–Roy Disney

This simple statement gives hope to everyone. Surviving and thriving in America has its share of challenges, but when we know our core values, we know what to do and how we need to do it.

We've already mentioned Collins and Porras's research showing the importance of preserving the core, where the "core" includes both core values and purpose. In *Good to Great,* as Jim Collins explains how *good* companies can make the leap to become *great* companies, he mentions core values in particular: "Core values are essential for enduring greatness," and we must take care to "preserve them over time."

I believe the same is true for our nation. Understanding and embracing our core values will have more impact on our American life than anything else.

Reflect to Connect

1. What guides your thinking and conduct?
2. What benefits result when people know and embrace a common set of core values?
3. Do you know who you are—bone deep?

Defining Core Values

So, what *are* core values? I like Jim Collins's definition of core values, which can apply equally well to an organization, our country, or an individual: "Core values are the organization's essential and enduring tenets—a small set of general guiding principles; not to be confused with specific cultural or operating practices; not to be compromised for financial gain or short-term expediency."

Core values answer the question, "Who are we?"

Core values require
- **Authenticity.** Getting real, with nothing added for public agreement.
- **Introspective reflection.** What do we stand for? What are we all about?
- **Articulating what is inside, bone deep.** Those things that are as natural as breathing.

Core values are *not* about figuring out what
- Maximizes your wealth.
- Sounds good to yourself or others.
- Reflects your aspirations.
- Complements a marketing campaign.
- Pleases the financial community.
- Looks attractive printed on glossy paper.
- Echoes popular or political opinion.
- Appeals to outsiders.

In *The 7 Habits of Highly Effective People,* Stephen Covey reveals one important characteristic of proactive people: they respond according to their values. In other words, when we know our core values, we respond to people based on who we are, rather than who they are or their condition. The same is true when we respond to circumstances—we respond based on who we are, not what the situation is. This allows us to make better decisions and make better decisions faster.

However, since most people do not know their core values, they react out of unpredictable emotions based on who the people are and also their condition. Therefore, they often make worse decisions and make worse decisions faster—sometimes causing chaos.

It All Starts with the Founders

Whether we're talking about a nation, organization, or business, the core values discovery process must begin with the founders. Over time, employees will come and go, but the founders and their legacy will remain.

Wait a minute: if the founders set the core values, does that mean individuals are being asked to ignore their own personal core values and simply take on the core values of their country's or company's founders?

Should thousands of employees alter their lives and behavior to match one person's set of values?

Absolutely not! As Jim Collins explained in *Built to Last* and *Good to Great*, the visionary companies that outperformed the stock market by fifteen times had founders who established their core values at the very beginning. They then went about recruiting, selecting, hiring, and onboarding employees who held the *same* core values. They hired the right people—those of like core values—and put them in the right positions.

They did not have employees with a diverse set of core values. Instead, they developed a unique, consistent culture of remarkable *unity*, one where people lived out a shared set of core values and purpose.

The same applies when our country clearly defines who we are and our core values guide all citizens, including those immigrating into our country, on how we should live.

Jim Collins also explained in *Built to Last* and *Good to Great* that the visionary companies had a cult-like culture with people authentically living out the *same* core values.

Even though we existed for decades before my company memorialized our core values, those values were always present. Why?

I was authentically living them out, even though I had not put them in writing. And our Human Resource department regularly hired people who fit what the leader (me) wanted in our organization.

When my company did hire an employee who did not truly share our core values, that new employee quickly learned that he or she did not fit in our organization and chose to leave. They weren't bad people; they just knew they did not fit. And our other employees knew it as well.

In chapter 1, I mentioned that our country's core values are freedom and responsibility. At this point, you may be asking, "Where did these core values come from?" In the next chapter, we will discuss how our country's core values were identified by our founders in the Declaration of Independence.

Your Personal Core Values

Much like a dropped object is controlled by the Law of Gravity, core values are subject to what we might call the Core Values' Law of Origin: the authentic core values of an organization originate and flow from the founder(s), and the leaders must continue to champion them, just like the leaders of our country must continue championing the American core values of

Freedom and Responsibility.

In addition to their nation's core values, every person also has personal core values. They may be separate from our nation's values, but they do not conflict with them. May I invite you to start the process of reflecting on your own life to discover your core values in light of our nation's values of freedom and responsibility?

At TFP-book.com, you can download a copy of the Core Values Discovery Guide, which includes questions to help you in the discovery process. There you can also download the Core Values Validator Worksheet to make sure the core values you've identified are real, true, and authentic to you.

Reflect to Connect

1. Do you know your core values?
2. If so, what role do they play in your decisions?
3. If not, do you find it difficult to identify an unchanging basis for your decision making?

The Blind Leading the Blind

How well do our country's leaders follow and promote our core values today? I believe it's safe to say that, in general, America's leaders do *not* know "who we are." As a result, the American people don't really know who they are either.

Often you will hear our country's leaders defend their own bias by saying this is or is not one of our core values; however, if you would ask them to explain the American core values, they would have difficulty explaining what they are.

In fact, most Americans couldn't tell you what our country's core values are or what they mean. We may have learned them once or twice during a short civic lesson in school or from our parents. But that's it—if we were lucky.

It is sad that most people today work hard every day and try to do the right thing. But they don't seem to get very far on the path toward "Life, Liberty, and the pursuit of Happiness." Worse, they don't even know *why*.

I believe the reason why is that we don't know who we are, and, therefore, we don't understand *how* we should behave when interacting with and communicating with one other. Without a common set of core values, there's a lack of cohesiveness and unity of spirit and little teamwork to make the American Dream work.

Neither are there systems in place to assure alignment of core values throughout our organizations and governmental offices. In fact, our nation's government entities, businesses, and/or non-profits (including churches) may well create laws, regulations, incentives, and encouragements that actually violate one or both of our core values. Later in this book, we will explore four cultural changes that have resulted from the violation of our country's core values of freedom *and* responsibility.

Freedom is only part of the story and half the truth . . .
That is why I recommend that the Statue of Liberty on the
East Coast be supplemented by a Statue of
Responsibility on the West Coast.
–Viktor E. Frankl

These organizations may be delivering okay results. But if our national, state, and local government entities and the American people were all aligned with the same core values, they could knock the ball out of the park.

A culture of discipline is not just about action. It is about
getting disciplined people who engage in disciplined thought
and who then take disciplined action.
–Jim Collins

Jim Collins is saying that when you have disciplined people—people who are intentional and guided by the *same* core values and purpose—you produce superior results.

And it starts with people knowing and fervently behaving according to the same core values.

Business leaders have learned that even more important than a powerful strategy, a super product, or the newest technology is an organization of people with the same core values—people who know *how* to behave as they pursue the organization's purpose, vision, mission, strategies, tactics, and measurable goals.

These organizations substantially outperform all others. And the same can be true of America.

As our leaders champion these core values, we as citizens can unite around a common core so that our country can also have a culture where people thrive and prosperity soars.

*Freedom makes a huge requirement of every human being.
With freedom comes responsibility. For the person who is
unwilling to grow up, the person who does not want to carry his
own weight, this is a frightening prospect.*
—Eleanor Roosevelt

Reflect to Connect

1. Have you gained a deeper understanding of America's core values?
2. Are you willing to live out the American core values?

Now that you understand what core values are, what they are not, and why they are important, we'll take a deeper look at the second part of what it means to preserve the core: knowing our purpose (why we exist).

CHAPTER FOUR:

America's Purpose: Religious Freedom

What History Reveals about Why America Exists

*When you're surrounded by people who share
a passionate commitment around a common purpose,
anything is possible.*

–Howard Schultz

William Bradford became a leading figure in the Puritans› Separatist Movement. He and other congregants eventually sailed from England on the *Mayflower* to establish a colony in Plymouth, Massachusetts, in 1620.

At one point in their voyage to the New World, a huge wave struck the side of the ship and strained "a structural timber until it had cracked like a chicken bone."[4] The captain was considering turning back to England, but Bradford and his friends protested. Using a screw jack they had brought for lifting heavy lumber, they stabilized the shattered beam. Their actions made it clear to all on board there would be no turning back.

The group of travelers would later be called the Pilgrims because of their quest to find religious freedom in the New World. Upon arrival in November 1620, Bradford signed the first set of laws for the colony called the Mayflower Compact with deep roots in English documents such as the Magna Carta.

The rule of law was primarily associated with the Common Law of England. The English also regarded God as the author of all law. One of the main concepts derived from the Mayflower Compact was governing law for and by the people. This concept is the heart of democracy.

More challenges, even heartache, awaited Bradford. He volunteered to join a group making expeditionary trips in search of a place to settle. Upon returning to the *Mayflower* after the third such trip, Bradford learned of the death of his wife, Mary, who fell overboard off the deck of the anchored ship and drowned.

Bradford persisted as a leader and was an influential Pilgrim figure. He led an active political life, serving as governor as well as in other political offices for the remainder of his life upon settling Plymouth Colony.

The Pilgrims' first winter was very hard, but in the spring, Native Americans of the Wampanoag Tribe taught them how to grow corn and catch fish. After a successful harvest, the Pilgrims invited the Wampanoag to join in a feast. Today we think of their celebration as the first Thanksgiving.

In the spring of 1630, John Winthrop sailed for Massachusetts aboard the *Arbella*. He was the first governor of the Massachusetts Bay Colony, in and around Boston, and a prominent figure among the Puritan founders of New England. Winthrop, a lawyer, was one of the best educated of the Puritan colonists. He had great leadership skills and wisdom and was known for being very religious.

John Winthrop described the colony as a "city on a hill" because he hoped that the Puritans in Massachusetts would become an example for other Christians around the world.

The Puritans, led by John Winthrop, came in search of prosperity and, like the Pilgrims, for religious and political freedom. The Puritans hoped to escape economic hardship and what they saw as worldly evils—corruption of churches and schools—in England and Europe. His legal mind joined his Puritan soul to craft a description of this city on a hill and how they could build it together. Winthrop's sermon, "A Model of Christian Charity," would call the people to sincere faith in God and warn them that their success or failure would be seen by all people.

William Bradford and John Winthrop risked everything to sail across the ocean to an unknown land for one purpose: religious freedom. They knew their "why," and it, in turn, fueled their passion, will, and determination to succeed.

Why Does America Exist?

Both Bradford and Winthrop put the highest priority on the freedom to worship and live as Christians in this new land without interference from the government.

Their desire to freely exercise their Christian faith was central to both of these men and to virtually all the Pilgrims and Puritans who followed them. This desire to express and live out their beliefs without government persecution or even oversight was the burning "why" that inspired and fueled their brave departure from England and their subsequent lives of influence in the new land.

Given this context of early America, it is easy to see that America exists for the purpose of "religious freedom," specifically as a Christian nation.

The reformation was preceded by the discovery of America, as if the Almighty graciously meant to open a sanctuary to the persecuted in future years, when home should afford neither friendship nor safety.
–Thomas Paine

You may ask, "Did people come to America for other reasons?" The answer is yes; for example, others came for economic opportunity.

However, even the pursuit of economic opportunity was rooted in Christian virtues, like diligence, industriousness, prudence, reliability, and a tendency to save in order to invest in the future.

The Declaration of Independence, adopted on July 4, 1776, in Philadelphia, established the principle that all are created equal and have the God-given right to live, to be free, and to pursue happiness.

Thirty-three-year-old Thomas Jefferson wrote the Declaration of Independence. The document clearly acknowledged the power of God, and it served as the Thirteen Colonies' instrument of separation from the power of the British Empire.

> *The God who gave us life gave us*
> *liberty at the same time.*
> **–Thomas Jefferson**

The Declaration of Independence did not offer a specific plan of government, but it did contain a pledge of unity and a name for the new country: the United States of America.

> *We hold these truths to be self-evident, that all men are*
> *created equal, that they are endowed by their Creator with*
> *certain unalienable Rights, that among these are Life, Liberty*
> *and the pursuit of Happiness–That to secure these rights,*
> *Governments are instituted among Men, deriving their just*
> *powers from the consent of the governed.*
> **–Declaration of Independence**

Let us explore three significant truths from these well-known words in the Declaration of Independence:

1. "We hold these truths to be self-evident, that all men are created equal, that they are endowed by their Creator."

All people are made (created) in the image of God (our Creator). "Equality" means all people, you and me, are treated the same with dignity, respect, and love by God. This equality serves as a starting point, offering equal opportunities to all citizens. It does not mean you have a right to equal outcomes. You are personally responsible for your own outcomes or what you do with the opportunities afforded you. You reap what you sow.

You make choices, and your choices make you.

2. "We hold these truths to be self-evident, that all men are created equal, that they are endowed by their Creator with certain unalienable Rights, that among these are Life, Liberty, and the pursuit of Happiness."

These "Rights" are a gift (endowed) from God (our Creator). They are not from human beings or from the government. Therefore, every individual person who receives these rights is accountable to the Giver of said rights. Thus, we are responsible to God to be obedient to His laws, precepts, and principles (truths that are self-evident). God is love, and at the same time, He is a just God.

Here we can clearly see our core values of freedom *and* responsibility. This is why the US Supreme Court is the last line of defense to ensure every American's "unalienable Rights" are protected from the government and, at the same time, to ensure Americans are obedient to our laws, which are rooted in God's precepts and principles.

3. "That to secure these rights, Governments are instituted among Men, deriving their just powers from the consent of the governed."

Fifty-six representatives from each of the Thirteen Colonies came together as one, the United States of America, unified to declare their independence from the tyrannical and oppressive king of Great Britain—a top-down government.

The Declaration of Independence set forth a government that was to serve the people (to secure these rights), rather than the people serving the government, thus defining a bottom-up structure of government.

America's government was to take on a servant leader's attitude—"to serve, not be served." The government had only the powers that the sovereign people delegated (or consented) to it.

> *When the people fear the government, there is tyranny. When the government fears the people, there is liberty.*
> **–Thomas Jefferson**

Those fifty-six representatives understood that the most efficient and effective government is one where Americans (the governed) are engaged to participate in the decision-making process, both top-down and bottom-up at the same time. It is a dialogue, not a monologue. This is possible when those who govern realize they receive their "just powers" from the "consent of the governed." When this occurs, trust exists between those in power and those they serve.

> *Four score and seven years ago our fathers brought forth on this continent, a new nation, conceived in Liberty, and dedicated to the proposition that all men are created equal . . . that this nation, under God, shall have a new birth of freedom— and that government of the people, by the people, for the people, shall not perish from the earth.*
> **–Abraham Lincoln**

Reflect to Connect

1. Have you ever connected America's purpose of religious freedom as a Christian nation and the Declaration of Independence?
2. Have you considered the differences between freedom of equal opportunities and responsibility of individual outcomes? In what ways have you changed your thinking about taking responsibility for your own outcomes?
3. How could you participate more in our government decision-making process?

What Has Been Said about America's Purpose?

But please don't take my word for it. Let's listen to what our Founding Fathers, American leaders, and even those outside of the United States have said about the purpose of our nation and the character of those who established it.

US Presidents

It is the duty of all nations to acknowledge the providence of Almighty God, to obey His will, to be grateful for His benefits, and humbly to implore His protection and favor.
—George Washington, Founding Father and first president of the United States

The liberty enjoyed by the people of these states of worshiping Almighty God agreeably to their conscience, is not only among the choicest of their blessings, but also of their rights.
—**George Washington,** annual meeting of Quakers, September 1789

Whereas it is the duty of all nations to acknowledge the providence of Almighty God, to obey His will, to be grateful for His benefits, and humbly to implore His protection and favor . . . that we may then all unite in rendering unto Him our sincere and humble thanks . . . unite in most humbly offering our prayers and supplications to the great Lord and Ruler of Nations.
—**George Washington,** Thanksgiving Proclamation, November 26, 1789

We have no government armed with power capable of contending with human passions unbridled by morality and religion . . . Our Constitution was made only for a moral and religious people. It is wholly inadequate to the government of any other.
—**John Adams,** Founding Father and second president of the United States

And can the liberties of a nation be thought secure when we have removed their only firm basis, a conviction in the minds of the people that these liberties are the gift of God? That they are not to be violated but with His wrath? Indeed, I tremble for my country when I reflect that God is just; that His justice cannot sleep forever.
—**Thomas Jefferson,** Founding Father and third president of the United States

Before any man can be considered as a member of civil society, he must be considered as a subject of the Governor of the Universe.
—**James Madison,** Founding Father and fourth president of the United States

Is it not that the Declaration of Independence first organized the social compact on the foundation of the Redeemer's mission upon earth? That it laid the cornerstone of human government upon the first precepts of Christianity?
—**John Quincy Adams,** sixth president of the United States

Freedom prospers when religion is vibrant and the rule of law under God is acknowledged.
—**Ronald Reagan,** fortieth president of the United States

Founding Fathers

To the kindly influence of Christianity, we owe that degree of civil freedom, and political and social happiness, which mankind now enjoys.
—**Jedidiah Morse,** Founding Father

I've lived, sir, a long time, and the longer I live, the more convincing proofs I see of this Truth: That God governs in the affairs of men. If a sparrow cannot fall to the ground without His notice, is it probable that an empire can rise without His aid? We've been assured, sir, in the sacred writings that "except the Lord builds the house, they labor in vain who build it."

I firmly believe this, and I also believe that without His concurring aid we shall succeed in this political building no better than the builders of Babel.
—**Benjamin Franklin,** Founding Father

Supreme Court Justices

The Bible is the best of all books, for it is the word of God and teaches us the way to be happy in this world and in the next. Continue therefore to read it and to regulate your life by its precepts.
—**John Jay,** first chief justice of the US Supreme Court

Providence has given to our people the choice of their rulers, and it is the duty, as well as the privilege and interest of our Christian nation, to select and prefer Christians for their rulers.
—**John Jay,** first chief justice of the US Supreme Court

Human law must rest its authority ultimately upon the authority of the law which is Divine.
—**James Wilson,** original justice of the US Supreme Court

Congress

We are a Christian people . . . not because the law demands it, not to gain exclusive benefits or to avoid legal disabilities, but from choice and education; and in a land thus universally Christian, what is to be expected, what desired, but that we shall pay due regard to Christianity?
—**Senate Judiciary Committee Report, January 19, 1853**

At the time of the adoption of the Constitution and the amendments, the universal sentiment was that Christianity should be encouraged . . . In this age there can be no substitute for Christianity . . . That was the religion of the founders of the republic and they expected it to remain the religion of their descendants.
—House Judiciary Committee Report, March 27, 1854

Educational Institutions

Let every student be plainly instructed and earnestly pressed to consider well the main end of his life and studies is to know God and Jesus Christ which is eternal life (John 17:3) and therefore to lay Christ in the bottom as the only foundation of all sound knowledge and learning. And seeing the Lord only giveth wisdom, let every one seriously set himself by prayer in secret to seek it of Him (Proverbs 2,3). Every one shall so exercise himself in reading the scriptures twice a day that he shall be ready to give such an account of his proficiency therein.
—Harvard 1636 student guidelines

All the scholars are required to live a religious and blameless life according to the rules of God's Word, diligently reading the Holy Scriptures, that fountain of Divine light and truth, and constantly attending all the duties of religion.
—Yale 1787 student guidelines

Foreign Opinion

The Americans combine the notions of Christianity and of liberty so intimately in their minds that it is impossible to make them conceive the one without the other.
—Alexis de Tocqueville, French observer of America in 1831, author of *Democracy in America*

There is no country in which the people are so religious as in the United States.
—Achille Murat, French observer of America in 1832

Further Testimony on the Christian Character of America

Throughout the past two centuries, our Founding Fathers and national leaders have been clear about our purpose of religious freedom as well as the uniquely Christian character of the United States of America (as a result of that religious freedom). Today, there are numerous religious symbols on edifices in and around the nation's capital that add their voices to that testimony.

Images and representations of the Bible, the crucifix, Moses, and the Ten Commandments exist in engravings and sculptures at the Washington Monument, the Jefferson and Lincoln Memorials, the Capitol building, the Library of Congress, the White House, the World War II Memorial, and Arlington National Cemetery.

At the Supreme Court, the Ten Commandments are displayed in no less than three places: over the east portico, on the court doors, and over the chief justice's chair. But there is one witness to America's religious heritage that many people carry in their purses and wallets: the one-dollar bill. Centered on the back of the dollar bill are the words, "In God We Trust."

These symbols confirm that the founders never intended to remove religion and religious people from government or from public life.

When our Founding Fathers passed the First Amendment, they sought to protect churches from government interference. They never intended to construct a wall of hostility between government and the concept of religious belief itself.
–Ronald Reagan

Reflect to Connect

1. Do you clearly know why America exists?
2. Are you willing to risk everything, like William Bradford and John Winthrop, to pursue America's purpose?
3. How much must our God-given right to religious freedom be threatened before we will boldly stand to acknowledge and defend it?

Many scholars have called James Madison the Father of the Constitution. When the Constitutional Convention began in Philadelphia in 1787, no other delegate was better prepared than Madison with his passion that fueled him to fight for religious freedom, America's purpose.

He'd already spent years researching and refining the concept of a government that separated the executive, legislative, and judicial powers. His proposals were the working model used by the Convention delegates.

Today, we can thank Madison for being the Founding Father who laid the foundation for religious freedom in our country. Because of him, the notion of the free exercise of religion became our national standard.

His lifelong efforts ensured that citizens had the right to live according to their deepest convictions without government interference and paved the way for Americans to freely and openly live out our faith.

James Madison was born March 16, 1751, in Virginia, to a wealthy family of plantation owners. He attended the College of New Jersey (later Princeton) and studied under Reverend John Witherspoon, who shaped Madison's view on the rights and freedoms of individuals as coming from God, not from man.

After completing his college education, Madison returned home to Montpelier, Virginia. At age twenty-five, he became a delegate to the Virginia Convention and vowed to advocate for legislation that would protect religious freedom for all.

In 1776, Madison worked on an important foundational document known as the Virginia Declaration of Rights, a precursor and model for the US Bill of Rights that would come years later.

Madison argued to truly protect the right of an individual to follow his conscience:

> *All men are equally entitled to enjoy*
> *the freedom of exercise of religion, according to*
> *the dictates of conscience.*

In 1786, Madison's political savvy and effective negotiation helped him succeed at ratifying the Virginia Statute of Religious Freedom, an important document Jefferson had written years earlier designed to protect religious liberty.

Three years later, as part of the battle to get the Constitution ratified by the Thirteen Colonies, Madison drafted the Bill of Rights, including what was to become the First Amendment.

Congress largely relied on Madison's original draft, and the states subsequently ratified two principles—"no establishment" and "free exercise"—that protect one freedom: religious freedom as a fundamental, inalienable right for every person.

The final version that we know today is written as follows:

Congress shall make no law respecting an establishment of religion, or prohibiting the free exercise thereof.

In addition to his passion for religious liberty, Madison underscored "conscience is the most sacred of all property."

Because religious rights were central to Madison's worldview, he saw the inherent link between freedom of conscience and freedom of religion.

Madison was convinced that keeping government out of the affairs of the church (or religion) was the only way that people could follow the dictates of their conscience.

He viewed established state religion as a denial of the fundamental, God-given right of conscience. Due to this, he concluded that the institution of the church should not be directed by the government in any way, a principle that was enshrined in his original draft of the First Amendment.[5]

Reflect to Connect

1. Did you know that James Madison had such an influential role in the creation of our constitution?

2. In what ways might America be different today if Madison had not fervently supported and defended our religious rights?

How America Preserved Its Core

In chapter 2, I wrote of how Jim Collins explained in *Built to Last* and *Good to Great* that the visionary companies that outperformed the stock market by fifteen times had founders who established their core values and purpose at the very beginning.

These companies' core ideology—core values and purpose—was so strong that they were known to have a cult-like culture, and it was fanatically protected and never changed (i.e., they preserved their core).

Madison's work on the First Amendment of the US Constitution provided a way to protect and preserve the American purpose of religious freedom. This purpose of religious freedom and the Christian character of the United States also served to preserve and protect our core values of freedom and responsibility.

For example, since the only textbook that generally existed in America during colonial times was the Bible (due to our religious *freedom*), families and schools used it to teach the standards of *responsibility*.

That is how people knew how to behave in a responsible and principled way. The deep Christian roots of our nation explain why our purpose and our understanding of how to behave responsibly are so closely aligned.

There is a foundational truth in the Bible: each person is responsible for their actions. More specifically, it says we are each responsible for our own wrongdoing or sin. In other words, my parents are not responsible for my wrongdoing; my boss is not responsible; the government is not responsible. I am responsible. But faith opens the door for us to receive freedom from the burden of our wrongdoing.

The Bible is a book ... which teaches man his own
individual responsibility, his own dignity, and his equality
with his fellow man.
–Daniel Webster

*Liberty cannot be established without morality,
nor morality without faith.*

–Alexis de Tocqueville

Also, American history records countless accounts of God's provision and protection. For example, in 1755, Colonel George Washington led a group Virginians, along with British troops, into battle during the French and Indian War, and they suffered enormous losses. Remarkably, George Washington was the only mounted officer not shot down off his horse, and he had been quite vulnerable to injury. Having accepted the responsibility to bolster and engage his troops, he bravely rode back and forth along the front lines. He had two horses shot from under him, yet he continued to lead with valor.

After arriving back at Fort Cumberland, he described what had occurred in battle—that when he had removed his jacket at the end of the battle, he discovered it bore four bullet holes but not a single bullet had touched him. The story of the divine protection of Washington spread across the colonies.

Just as all citizens have unique, individual core values that are compatible with our nation's core values, we also have a unique, personal life purpose that is compatible with our nation's purpose. However, in my experience coaching and consulting with leaders, I have found that while most people easily understand the importance of core values, they have a harder time understanding the importance of discovering their purpose.

Why? Well, that's exactly the right question to ask.

In the next chapter, I hope to convince you that discovering your personal "why" is one of the most important things you can do—not only for yourself but for our nation.

CHAPTER FIVE:

Discover Your Life Purpose

Know Your Why to Find Your Way

When I found my why, I found my way.
When I found my why, I found my will.
When I found my why, I found my wings.
—John Maxwell

Bradford and Winthrop knew their why, and it fueled their passion, will, and determination to succeed. To know your why, you must *ask* why—a question many people in this country seem to have forgotten how to ask.

Why Do Americans Stop Asking Why?

"Why" is a question we all ask naturally as children. If you've ever been around kids, I'm sure you have experienced this. In fact, sometimes their insistent why questions seem a bit like the drip, drip, drip of water torture. But don't be so quick to shun this simple practice.

Everyone can learn more by adopting and encouraging the childlike practice of asking why.

Why do children ask why so often? Between the ages of two and three, children develop the cognitive ability to make logical connections, and this advance sparks the following behavior:

- Curiosity and eagerness to explore this fascinating world
- Desire to explore with the people they feel the safest around and love the most
- Drive to learn and understand why things happen
- Push to ask why, which reflects a thirst for knowledge
- Use of new critical skills that help them gain a much more complex understanding of how the world works, via what they see, hear, and do
- Understanding that the more they ask why, the more they learn

Unfortunately this curiosity doesn't last. A *Newsweek* story, "The Creativity Crisis," described the signs of declining creativity among our school children.[6] The article cited an interesting fact that preschool kids ask their parents an average of one hundred questions a day. Wow! However, by middle school, they've basically stopped asking questions. It is also around this time that student motivation and engagement drop like a rock.

If kids get so many benefits from asking why, why do they eventually stop? Apparently because our educational system rewarded students for having the answer, not for asking good questions. We have an answers-driven school system.

Knowing the answers to questions will help you in school. Knowing how to ask questions will help you in life.
–Warren Berger

I'd like to invite you to think like a child again and learn how to ask the most important question: why?

Why Is Greater than What and How

School children eventually grow up into adults (us), and that's why many of us have a hard time thinking about our purpose in life—*why* we do what we do. In our answer-driven society, we find it much easier to ask the questions "what" and "how." For example, it's easier to ask yourself, "What new car would I like to own, and how could I purchase it?" than "Why do I think my current vehicle is inadequate?" Or in business, we tend to focus on the strategic "what" questions, such as "What do we want to accomplish?" and the tactical "how" questions, such as "How can we make that happen most efficiently?"

Both strategy and tactics are important. However, those who really make a difference ask why first and then go on to figure out the best what and how. The "why" enables you to find the best "whats" and "hows" because the why provides the *passion* for what you are doing.

For example, in most organizations, the bosses figure out the what and how and employees do what they're told. However, that thinking is counterproductive, because those employees don't know *why* they're doing what they are doing. And the why provides the motivation.

After all, people on the front line can often bring better ideas forward because they see what works in practice and are willing to challenge traditional practices. Innovation and creativity are not the exclusive domain of leadership.

We should pay attention to those who respectfully ask why because they are demonstrating an interest in their work and exhibiting a curiosity that could position them as future leaders of their organization or even our country.

Reflect to Connect

1. Have you stopped asking why?
2. How could we as citizens be encouraged to ask *why* we are doing things more often?

Is Your Why Big Enough to Succeed?

According to the Small Business Administration, approximately two-thirds of businesses survive at least two years, about half survive at least five years, and only a third survive at least ten years.

Business failure rates have much to do with leaders not honestly asking the why question of themselves. Instead, these leaders assume the leadership role without the passion and professional will their organization needs to succeed for the decades to come. The same holds true for America.

Think about it. If the leader lacks passion and professional will, how do you think the employees are going to behave after watching the leader? The leaders of a nation have a similarly powerful impact on their citizens. And you have the same impact on the people who look up to you.

People do what people see.
–John Maxwell

Do you want our nation to thrive? Everyone can help our nation stay the course by overcoming one challenge: embracing a why that is large enough to carry themselves and America forward. We must ask ourselves:

- Is my why bigger than me?
- Is my why bigger than my life in America, my current business, or current job responsibilities?

Reflect to Connect

1. How strong is your why?
2. Is your why bigger than you?

Asking why is not just an academic question; it has bottom-line results. In a study done at the University of Pennsylvania's Wharton School of Business, researchers divided employees at the university call center, where they solicited donations from alumni, into three groups. Each group was prepped for making calls in a different way:

- Group one interacted in person with beneficiaries of the donations.
- Group two read stories from beneficiaries about how the donations helped them with their education, careers, and lives.
- Group three had no contact at all with the beneficiaries.

After a month of calling, researchers found that group one raised significantly more money than the other groups.

Group one's deeper understanding of the impact of their work on students who benefitted from the money raised—the why—motivated them to get better results. What you do and how you do it are important, but the why provides the passion and energy to succeed.

The person who knows "how" will always have a job.
The person who knows "why" will always be his boss.
–Diane Ravitch

Only when people find their why deep within will they have the passion and professional will to resolve to do whatever it takes to thrive, no matter how big or hard the decision.

How do you know if your why is strong enough? Ask yourself these questions:

- Is passion a characteristic of my life?
- Do I wake up feeling enthusiastic about my day?
- Is the first day of the week my favorite, or do I live from weekend to weekend, sleepwalking through my everyday routine?
- How long has it been since I couldn't sleep because I was too excited by an idea?

Does your passion show? To get an honest assessment, just ask your coworkers or a friend. Ask your spouse about your level of desire.

Reflect to Connect

1. Is passion a characteristic of your life?
2. If an American leader left their position today, would "We the People" understand why America exists well enough to continue on?

What Is Your Why?

Have you ever considered why you do what you do each day? Why do you get out of bed? Do you get up and do what's necessary to simply receive a paycheck? Or, is there something bigger happening?

Are you too busy building a career or a business and trying to become financially secure? Is your work the center of your identity and life? Are you rushing around without a life purpose?

Are you forever talking about the Promised Land, but you can't bring yourself to leave your familiar territory—a known place that feels like home, even if not a great one?

Do you hear that still, small voice telling you to move on to something better, but you regularly push it aside? You know that voice is true, but you also know that to follow it would lead you into unfamiliar, uncharted territory.

Do you keep telling yourself any of these lines?

- "It would be better to wait until I'm finished with what I'm doing."
- "I'm too tired."
- "I'll do it someday" (knowing that "someday" never seems to come).

One day I discovered that my calendar was filled with activity but not necessarily accomplishment. Finding my life purpose helped me prioritize where to apply my time, talent, and treasures.

Once you understand your life purpose, you will prioritize your life according to that purpose. Without a clear life purpose, you'll get off track, and you may never feel a real sense of fulfillment and completion.

A person with a clear purpose will make progress, even on the roughest road. A person with no purpose will make no progress, even on the smoothest road.

–Thomas Carlyle

Reflect to Connect

1. Do you know why you exist?
2. Are you rushing around without a life purpose?
3. What are the benefits of taking time to pause, reflect, and evaluate your life?

Ask Why Now, Reap Eight Benefits Later

Imagine embracing a life filled with curiosity. What if we cultivated a joy for exploring? What if we became fascinated with the world around us and had a thirst to learn more every day? The childlike quality of asking why will enable us to think and live with more intention.

I don't just want knowledge; I want understanding.

Every person who asks why will enjoy the following eight benefits.

1. You will understand who you are.

As you go through your day with your antenna up, continually observe and ask yourself the following questions:

- Why did I say what I just said?
- Why was it important for me to say it that way?
- Why did I do what I just did?
- Why was it important for me to do it that way?

The power of these why questions will make you more aware of your actions and teach you more about yourself—your motives and purposes in life.

2. You will know where you are going.

Do you know where you are headed? Why or why not? Are you comfortable being on autopilot, doing the same thing with the same people and talking about the same things?

If you do what you've always done,
you'll get what you've always gotten.
–Tony Robbins

Are you doing what you love doing? Have you asked why? Are you where you want to be in life? Have you asked why? Your answer to your why question may just take you in a new direction.

3. You will recover your passion.

Why is passion so important? You can either surrender to your circumstances, or you can surrender to a cause that is so great, your circumstances won't matter.

When you surrender to your circumstances, you will have good days and bad days. You are at the mercy of what happens *to* you. But, when you surrender to a cause or purpose, you have good days wherever you go.

The purpose never dies. Your passion will help you conclude that it didn't matter what happened *to* you so long as the purpose continues because it is all about what has happened *in* you.

Passion is the fuel for the will. When you discover what you want and want it badly enough, you can find the willpower to achieve it. And, you are a more dedicated and productive person.

A leader with great passion and few skills always outperforms a leader with great skills and no passion.
–John Maxwell

Passion also gives you energy and credibility. When you love what you do and do what you love, others find it inspiring. Do you know anyone who became successful at something they hate?

Success is waking up in the morning, whoever you are, wherever you are, however old or young, and bounding out of bed because there's something out there that you love to do, that you believe in, that you're good at–

*something that's bigger than you are, and you can hardly
wait to get at it again today.*
–Whit Hobbs

That's what passion does for you. Passion in you is compelling to others, and people want to follow people who are passionate.

4. You will make progress.

Purpose gives you drive. It shows you a destination. It paints a picture of your future. It energizes you. And it makes obstacles and problems seem small in comparison to its importance. All of this results in *progress.*

Without a clear life purpose, you'll continually get off track, and you may never feel a real sense of fulfillment and completion. Once you understand your life purpose, you will prioritize your life according to that purpose, and those important goals that once seemed so elusive will finally get done.

*If you have a purpose in which you can believe, there's no end
to the amount of things you can accomplish.*
–Marian Anderson

5. You will achieve new levels of significance.

I don't know about you, but I want to make a difference.

*I want to make a difference in people, for people,
and through people.*

When you want to make a difference, you become a catalyst for change in people, in America, and in this world. When you ask why, you are asking because it matters, and the answer will shape what you do next.

Many times, asking why will lead to new ways you can help others. Also, asking why about important topics will highlight them, bring awareness, and instigate change that can make a difference.

6. You will face your fears.

Do you regularly avoid asking yourself the why question out of faith or fear? Do you have an unhealthy habit, behavior, or relationship? Why do you continue? Do you avoid the why question at all costs because you already know the answer or you feel guilty?

Does fear stop you from asking that vital question? Does this reluctance hinder you rather than help you develop relationships?

When you ask why, you're looking at your life under a microscope, which will help you deal with whatever fear or pain you hold deep within.

As you face your fears and thoughtfully ask why, you can evaluate your life with honesty and respect. This positions you to take your next step in faith instead of fear.

7. You will enhance your relationships.

When you show genuine interest in another person, you make that person feel important and worthy. And one of the best ways to encourage a good intellectual conversation and lift up the other person is to ask the question why. Why do they do what they do? Why do they enjoy what they enjoy?

Doing this stimulates enthusiasm and motivation in the other person. Most of all, you learn a lot more about him or her.

Asking questions and listening does more to enhance relationships than we think. Almost always, the person answering the questions comes away feeling you are a wonderful person to know, even though all you did was ask questions and listen.

8. You will add value to others.

When you openly and respectfully challenge yourself with the why question, it will inspire others to do the same.

When others see that you are growing and progressing through life because of your curiosity and fearlessness, they will want to have the same kind of life. It will encourage and inspire others to get what they want out of life, too.

You can start by asking the most important question: why.

Reflect to Connect

1. Are you ready to continually ask the question why?
2. Which of the eight benefits listed above will you claim today by intentionally asking why?

For a why strong enough to succeed, I have found that leaders need to take the time to discover both their personal life purpose and their organization's purpose. And it holds true for the leaders of our nation. Why? Because as a leader, their life purpose also affects the lives of the people around them.

Even if you are not a leader of a business or an organization, as an American citizen, you are still a leader. Every member of a democracy is a citizen leader because we have the freedom and responsibility to choose our leaders. That means we have a responsibility to know our life purpose as well as our nation's purpose.

If your why doesn't seem strong enough for your life, then it's time to find one that is.

So, let's lead ourselves first and discover our life purpose.

Time to Pause, Reflect, and Evaluate

Knowing your life purpose is like knowing your true north in every area of your life. It serves to properly orient you, even if your circumstances and surroundings change. It sets you on the course from success to significance.

I've developed a process to help you discover your personal why. What's important is that you don't give up until you find your life purpose.

Your life purpose is the reason why you were uniquely made and placed on this planet. When you discover it, it is like a beacon that shows the way in every area of your life.

It's time to listen to your inner voice. It is time to take stock, listen, and learn.

Stop rushing around. Pause, reflect, and evaluate your life so that you are ready to listen to that interior voice and discover why you exist, your life purpose.

Reflect to Connect

1. Do you know why you exist?
2. Are you rushing around without a life purpose?
3. Will you take time to pause, reflect, and evaluate?

I've prepared a special resource to help you discover your life purpose. You can download my Life Purpose Discovery Worksheet at TFP-book.com.

Once I discovered my life purpose, the first question I asked myself was, "Now what?" That is when I realized I needed to start living my life purpose.

So, the next logical question was, "How do I live out my life purpose?" Every successful life purpose needs some structure and an agenda to act upon.

Your life purpose is not something you want to do, but something you have to do. It is why you exist.

Every person has their own unique, personal life purpose, separate from our nation's purpose, but they do not conflict with each other. We pursue both at the same time—our life purpose *and* our American purpose.

Unfortunately, if you look at our culture as a whole, we aren't doing such a great job of living our national core values and purpose.

Specifically, I've noticed four cultural changes that are quickly eroding the founding principle of responsibility and, therefore, are threatening the promise of "Life, Liberty, and the pursuit of Happiness" in our great nation. They include the shift from:

1. Principled behavior to expedient behavior
2. An abundant mindset to a scarcity mindset
3. Focusing on root causes to focusing on symptoms
4. Valuing process *and* content (not just what we say and do but *how* we say and do it) to valuing content alone (what we say and do)

We'll begin with the most foundational: the cultural shift from principled to expedient behavior.

PART TWO

Freedom without Responsibility: Four Cultural Changes

CHAPTER SIX:

Principled versus Expedient Behavior

Do You Live by Intention or Impulse?

Our behavior is governed by principles. Living in harmony with them brings positive consequences; violating them brings negative consequences.

—Stephen Covey

As a young man, George Washington applied himself to farming and surveying, making the most of what he had.

During the French and Indian War, he won the military reputation of a leader who employed clever strategy to spend as few lives as possible, who expected discipline and hard work from his men, and who led his troops with intelligence and fearlessness.

By the time the Continental Congress needed a leader for the new American Army, there was no better choice than George Washington.

In Valley Forge, Washington trained his men and fought for them to get proper food and clothing and pay. In fact, he experienced the same cold, hunger, and exhaustion his men faced. He risked losing everything he had—land, fortune, and life—by opposing the British publicly.

*Our poor brave fellows living in tents, bare-footed,
bare-legged, bare-breeches . . . Nothing but virtue has kept
our army together.*
–Colonel John Brooks

Washington grew into a calm, measured, reasonable, courageous statesman who gave his utmost for the country's good. He served as long as he was needed, and when his term as president was over, he set the example of the peaceful transition of power that we still enjoy in America today. Had our first steward of liberty been another kind of man with another kind of mindset, our entire history could have been very different indeed.[7]

As a leader, George Washington clearly exhibited *principled* behavior. A person who exhibits principled behavior believes that today's short-term pain, sacrifice, and investment of time, energy, and money will eventually bring long-term growth, blessings, and success.

Principled behavior is rooted in *faith* and, as such, aligns you with time-tested ways to methodically create a successful life.

In contrast, let's take a look at another early American figure.

If you had looked only at Benedict Arnold's early career, you would be justified in your admiration. A prosperous Connecticut merchant, Arnold not only ran a solid business, but he also personally commanded the ships that carried goods along the American coast from Canada to the Caribbean and across the ocean to London.

He used that naval experience to help him capture Fort Ticonderoga from the British in the early days of the Revolution and to form the beginnings of an American navy on Lake Champlain.

So, where did he go so wrong? How could he go from trusted friend of George Washington to the most notorious traitor in American history? Once you look at the boy behind the man, you can begin to see the cracks in the foundation.

The Arnold family came over with the Puritans and settled in Rhode Island, where they came to prominence. But by the time Arnold's father reached manhood, little remained of that prominence but the name. Arnold's father worked his way up in a shipping business, marrying his master's rich widow when the man died. During the boom years right before the French and Indian War, the business prospered but failed soon afterward.

Buried in debt, Arnold's father turned to drinking and lost everything he had: money, prestige, and independence. He ended up in prison for debt and public drunkenness. What does such failure do to the heart of his son?

Benedict Arnold became an apprentice to his Uncle Lathrop, who welcomed him as a son. From this uncle, Arnold learned good business practices. But Benedict did not apply himself steadily.

Benedict did well in war. Brave, smart, and handsome, he won the notice of George Washington and the respect of the leaders of Connecticut, and when the Revolution started, they entrusted him with orders to capture Fort Ticonderoga.

However, Arnold soon showed himself sensitive to slights on his honor. After the accounting of what he had spent personally on the war effort was questioned, Arnold resigned his commission in a huff, only to ask for it back when another man led the expedition to Canada that Arnold had planned.

Passed over other times for promotions and recognition, even after suffering a wound in his leg, Arnold complained to George Washington. Still, George Washington liked him and put him in charge of Philadelphia. Then Congress questioned Arnold's financial dealings as a military leader in Philadelphia.

Benedict Arnold was brave and smart, a good soldier. But greed for money, so that he might never end up as a bankrupt like his father, and a fragile ego, which could not bear an insult, damaged the gifts he could have given his nation.

It was no wonder that he was commissioned in the British army. Unlike the American fight for liberty, the British struggle for power could offer Arnold all he truly wanted. Preoccupied with disappointments and personal conflicts, he chose an expedient solution over the principled path of loyalty, and America lost.[8]

> *Arnold has betrayed us! Whom can we trust now?*
> **–George Washington**

People who behave *expediently* do what's easiest and quickest or what makes them the happiest in the short run. They tend to make emotional decisions that are reactive in nature. Deep down, expedient behavior is most often rooted in *fear*. Such behavior eventually leads to undesirable results and negative consequences—even addiction or death.

Understanding principled versus expedient behavior is foundational to the three cultural changes that follow, so we're going to spend two chapters on this topic. In this chapter, we'll explore and clarify the important differences between these two approaches so you'll understand the painful pitfalls of emotion-driven expedient behavior and the immense benefits of character-driven principled behavior. We'll also explore some examples of principled versus expedient behavior in our culture. Then, in chapter 7, you'll learn how to apply this principle to your own life.

Reflect to Connect

1. Are you more principled or more expedient in your behavior?
2. How would you describe the behavior of George Washington?
3. Can you see Benedict Arnold as one who behaves expediently?

What Are Principled Behaviors?

Every person can identify principled behaviors through the following characteristics and results. Principled behaviors are actions based on the following:

- Fundamental beliefs and rules of conduct
- Long-term appropriateness and effectiveness
- Self-discipline and willingness to forgo the lure of immediate gratification or tempting shortcuts

The following are characteristics of principled behavior:

- More time consuming
- Team centered, focused on *we*
- Analytic
- Proactive
- Intentional
- Sacrificial in the short term
- Painful in the short term
- Worthwhile in the long term
- Secure

Again, principled behavior is rooted in *faith*—faith that what you want to happen is going to happen, and faith in the process that will produce long-term success.

Where there is faith, there is no fear.
And where there is fear, there is no faith.

The Results of Principled Behavior

When you consistently make principled decisions, you will eventually experience growth and success. And when the people and leaders of the United States exhibit principled behavior and employ principled decision-making, our country will also experience growth and success. Specifically, principled behavior results in the following:

- Sound decisions
- Reduced risks
- Fewer errors
- Less rework
- Continual progress
- Lasting gratification
- Enjoyment and fun
- Less stress
- Respect from and for others

Reflect to Connect

1. Are you willing to incur short-term pain, sacrifice, and the investment of time, energy, and money to behave in a principled way?
2. When you do behave in a principled way, have you found that it eventually brings long-term growth, blessing, and success?

What Are Expedient Behaviors?

Have you ever made a bad decision? When the mistake became obvious, did you have to spend a lot of time afterwards "mending fences" (i.e., dealing with the negative impact of your decision)?

I have made many. Even though I never have had a bad decision ruin my life, each time I've thought quite a bit about what went wrong. I believe that the root cause of our bad decisions usually comes down to expedient behavior.

Expedient behaviors are those that fulfill a person's immediate self-interests. They are done without consideration of what is just, fair, or right for the long term.

Expedient behavior has the following characteristics:

- Seems quick and easy
- Is self-centered, focused on *me*
- Provides short-term pleasure
- Reactive to the current situation
- Offers short-term gain
- Gives immediate gratification
- Is based on anxiety and insecurity
- Often indicates the pride of the person making the decision

Please keep in mind that expedient behavior is rooted in *fear*—the fear that you are going to lose something you don't want to lose or the fear that you are going to experience something you don't want to experience.

The Results of Expedient Behavior

When expedient behavior becomes a habit, you, those around you, and our country as a whole suffer unhealthy consequences. The following are examples of the results of expediency:

- Many unforeseen errors are found.
- The decision maker(s) and others must rework to find yet another solution.
- Other important priorities are neglected.
- Others affected by the expedient decision(s) complain about the consequences.
- Conflict arises because of unforeseen complications.
- The decision-maker(s) often experience regret for the expedient decision.
- The outcome fails entirely.

When these unhealthy consequences occur, do you "blow them off" with excuses by blaming someone or something else? Or do you learn from them and change to a principled way of behavior so you can move forward?

Principled behavior may take a little more time and a little more personal restraint, but principled behaviors almost always produce better results than expedient ones.

Reflect to Connect

1. How often do you find yourself "mending fences" due to expedient behavior?
2. Are you learning from your failures so you can move forward?

In every moment of every day, we are making choices. We have a choice to behave in an expedient way or in a principled way. We can choose to *play now* (in an expedient way) and pay more later or *pay now* (in a principled way) and play more later. Either way you choose, you still pay.

We make choices, and our choices make us.

In fact, much like the concept of compounding interest, if you choose to play now and pay later, you will pay *more* later. The choice is clear.

Though we have the freedom to make choices, we are not free to choose the consequences of our choices.

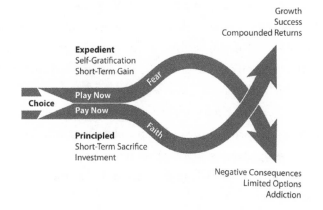

We must all suffer one of two things: the pain of discipline or the pain of regret or disappointment.

–Jim Rohn

Reflect to Connect

1. Do you mostly behave out of fear or faith?
2. Which do you prefer: to play now and pay more later or to pay now and play more later?
3. How can you prepare yourself to choose principled thinking and its benefits rather than the empty promises of expedient thinking?

Outside-In or Inside-Out?

When we choose principled behavior, we understand that we are personally responsible for our own lives. We do not blame people, circumstances, or environments.

This behavior is a product of our choices driven by our core values and purpose, rather than on conditions driven by *feelings*. Through principled behavior, people begin to work on the things they *can* do something about. By working on themselves instead of worrying about external conditions, they are able to even influence those conditions.

In other words, if you really want to improve your situation, the most positive way you can influence your situation is to work on the one thing over which you have control: *you*.

Those who exhibit *expedient* behaviors wait for something to happen or someone to take care of them. But people with *principled* behaviors achieve success by creating *proactive* solutions to their problems. They seize opportunities to do whatever it takes to get the job done in a principled way.

People with expedient behaviors have a paradigm that is "outside-in." They tell themselves that what's out there has to change before I can change.

People with principled behaviors have a paradigm that is "inside-out." They tell themselves they can have an effective, positive change on what's out there by working on *being* who they are (living out their core values and purpose). Living your core values means treating people not according to who *they* are but who *you* are.

Those who are principled think about what is right in the long run. They are self-disciplined to do what is right, even though it might not be the easiest or the quickest or the most enjoyable thing to do.

In short, principled, character-driven people are willing to do things emotion-driven people will not bother to do. Character-driven people enjoy long-term success while expedient, emotion-driven people usually wind up on the road to failure.

People who behave in a principled way make better decisions and better decisions faster as they seek what is right and then hold to those convictions. Because they are pro-active, they focus on what is important versus merely what is urgent.

Reflect to Connect

1. Are you taking responsibility for your choices without blaming others?
2. Is there one decision that you're considering today that you can approach in a more principled way? How so?

Recognizing Principled
and Expedient Behaviors

Do you like eating Krispy Kreme donuts? They are lip-smacking good. Have you ever eaten a Krispy Kreme donut when it comes out fresh and is still warm? They literally melt in your mouth.

Eating a donut requires little discipline. You simply pick your favorite donut (or three), pay for it, and enjoy the deliciousness. It is an expedient, emotional experience—until you weigh in the next day.

Because I love to eat and because I need a stress reliever, I've made a principled decision to stay active on a regular basis. In fact, I've been exercising six days a week, almost every week, for over thirty-eight years.

I have ridden my bicycle about a hundred thousand miles. I've sweated off countless calories while swimming and running. I even tried CrossFit. These days, I just focus on bicycling and long walks.

Discipline is doing what you don't want to do today so you can do what you want to do tomorrow.

Donut eating and regular exercise are perhaps obvious examples of expedient and principled behavior. But most of the situations we encounter present us with a choice to act in either an expedient or a principled way. Consider the following examples.

Personal Examples

Expedient: Interrupting others early and frequently without trying to understand what they are saying.

Principled: Listening to others without interrupting.

Expedient: Postponing or avoiding periodic checkups and preventive activities because you have other, more pleasant priorities.

Principled: Taking care of your health and your possessions, with periodic physicals for you and oil changes for your vehicles.

Expedient: Doing what you feel like doing until you risk being late and then speeding down streets and through intersections to arrive at a scheduled event.

Principled: Allowing ample time to drive to your destination safely.

Business Examples

In human resources:

Expedient: Hiring in haste and regretting at leisure.

Principled: Screening applicants carefully and always checking references.

Expedient: Taking a new employee to his or her desk, briefly describing duties, and going back to your daily tasks.

Principled: Providing new employees with ample guidance before giving them assignments.

Expedient: Making quick and easy promises to employees without verifying that the promises can be fulfilled without violating company policies and procedures.

Principled: Checking with your own supervisor before promising or doing anything for a subordinate regarding his or her employment.

In business meetings:

Expedient: Arriving for meetings at your convenience.

Principled: Considerately arriving on time so others aren't delayed.

Expedient: Holding meetings without prior information about the purpose of the meeting.

Principled: Announcing the purpose of the meeting along with the time and place.

In customer relations:
Expedient: Making unrealistic commitments to customers in order to get their agreement to buy.
Principled: Being clear and forthright with customers and prospects regarding the nature and timing of deliverables.

In leading and managing:
Expedient: Fire, ready, aim!
Principled: Ready, aim, fire!

Expedient: Continually reacting quickly when things go wrong (repetitively).
Principled: Tracking and analyzing patterns of problematic occurrences and designing preventive measures.

Expedient: Deciding or doing something quickly without checking with others.
Principled: When facing a challenge or opportunity, immediately seeking out people who can help you make a better decision, will have to carry out the decision, or will be impacted by it.

Expedient: As a supervisor or key staff member, doing everything you can in order to stay in control and be sure things are done to your liking.
Principled: Delegating to others whenever possible, even though you probably could do it more quickly—and more to your liking—by yourself.

Expedient: Orally giving the same instructions repeatedly each time a challenge or opportunity arises.

Principled: Investing the time to develop helpful systems, procedures, and checklists for repetitive future use.

The above examples of principled decisions require the *faith* and *discipline* to invest in appropriate communication, coordination, and cooperation with others, but the rewards are growth and success.

Reflect to Connect

1. Do you like eating donuts? If so, do you exercise to offset the calories?
2. Do you have the consistent discipline to make principled decisions?
3. Which example of principled behavior above are you going to put into practice?

Examples of Expedient Behavior in America

Although we can easily list examples of both principled behavior and expedient behavior in business and our personal lives, when we think about American cultural and political examples of principled behavior, they are few and far between.

The expedient behaviors and attitudes in our nation today have contributed to our loss of hope and lack of stability.

The lure of expedient thinking and actions has become almost too appealing for our society to resist. We have ditched responsibility in our short-sighted race to results. Unfortunately, the promises of expediency create their own problems.

*Our behavior is governed by principles. Living in harmony
with them brings positive consequences; violating them
brings negative consequences.*
–Stephen Covey

Here are some examples of expedient behaviors easily seen in American culture and politics:

Sound Bites

To make informed decisions, we need the truth, and the truth has become far more difficult to discern.

With our exhaustive 24/7 news cycle, everything moves fast, and we talk about the scandal of the hour. Media organizations are so desperately trying to hold on to us as an audience that they expediently make everything a mountain, nothing a molehill. The result is outrage fatigue. In pursuit of our attention at all cost, these organizations have abandoned the principled approach of accurate and balanced news coverage.

We learn in an expedient way, through sensational, emotional pictures and sounds and quick, shallow reads—like zipping along the surface on a jet ski.

To make wise decisions, we need to understand the deeper meaning of the issues and motivations of the media.

As long as "We the People" of this wonderful country continue to rely on quick and easy sound bites of news and information, we will continue to let expediency hide and distort the truth. The facts will only surface when we dig deeper into what is being said and why.

Media, Arts, and Entertainment

Industry leaders' expedient drive for profits for their shareholders and for themselves expose us and our children to what our eyes should not see and what our ears should not hear.

They lack responsibility because they choose to expose people to what stimulates the pleasure center in the brain, which increases our desire for more stimulation, like an addiction, so they can earn more profits for their shareholders and themselves.

They say that the parents are responsible for controlling what their children are being exposed to, which, at first blush, we think, "Yep, that's right." But when did the entertainment industry embrace values and principles that necessitate parents becoming media police in order to protect their kids from enticing choices that are extremely destructive?

The only thing necessary for the triumph of evil is for good men to do nothing.
–Edmund Burke

If It Is Legal, Is It Moral?

When people confuse what is legal with what is moral, everyone looks for a loophole to expediently serve their own self-interest. In the case of the media, arts, entertainment, food, and other industries, the focus is on money ("the love of money is a root of all kinds of evil"), without regard to the boundaries defined by integrity and responsibility. That is irresponsible capitalism.

The truth is that people are asking, "How low can I go?"

Neither the wisest constitution nor the wisest laws will secure the liberty and happiness of a people whose manners are universally corrupt . . . if we would most truly enjoy this gift of Heaven, let us become a virtuous people.
–Samuel Adams

One example is our college student loan system. College tuition has soared 1,375 percent since 1978, more than four times the rate of overall inflation, Labor Department data shows. Meanwhile, college presidents are being handsomely rewarded for the success of their enterprises. Seventy presidents earned over one million dollars in 2016–17, according to the *Chronicle of Higher Education*.

The federal student loan system gave colleges an incentive to maximize the tuition they extracted from students and the federal taxpayer by boosting fees and enrollment, which meant relaxing admissions standards along with increasing loan limits and grants.

Colleges could raise money quickly by admitting academically suspect students while suffering little or no consequences if their students dropped out and defaulted on loans.

And Sallie Mae and the private banks that fronted students the money for the federal student loan program made big profits as schools collected more money.

Laws and regulations are the minimum requirement for behavior, not a prescribed formula for success.

When we fail to ask, "Is it the right thing to do?" we soon find ourselves walking down the dark alley of expediency, with no light from guiding principles to show the way.

Reflect to Connect

1. How do you consume the daily news? Do you skim across the surface or dive deep to understand the real issues?

2. Have you seen recent examples of expedient, irresponsible behavior in the areas of arts and entertainment?

3. Do you know of someone who has asked, "Is it legal?" but not, "Is it moral?"

Technology

Who would had ever thought we would be talking about how giant technology companies are controlling our lives? These industry leaders' expedient drive for profits for their shareholders and for themselves exposes adults and our children to the following:

Exploitative business models. Powerful digital advertising platforms undermine user privacy and incentivize disinformation campaigns. The latest business models are based on acquiring, leveraging, and selling our personal information. Therefore, the user becomes the product.

Algorithms and artificial intelligence. Have you ever visited a website or purchased (or considered purchasing) a product or service, and days later when you visited another website, an ad appeared from that website you visited or from that product or service you purchased? Were you amazed at the accuracy of this activity-based marketing?

- These technology companies used algorithms and artificial intelligence to direct organizations, who paid them advertising fees, to target you as a potential revenue and profit source.

- These technology companies also use algorithms and artificial intelligence to search past comments you made, videos you uploaded, and documents you posted. They even chronicle your viewing of other people's comments, videos, and documents in order to direct you to people or groupswith similar interests.

- Therefore, these technology companies are accelerating the pace at which people sink deeper and deeper toward tribalism, extremism, resentment, and extreme radicalization. The results, though unintended, can be devastating. These companies are fueling mass violence by those who feel powerless, isolated, and lonely—seeking to discover meaning and fulfillment. In some cases, the more harm their extreme actions cause, the more significant an individual can feel.

- This technology is further "dividing" America. It is creating the same isolation and loneliness we feel as the last kid picked for kickball, which results in a natural desire to be part of a group. None of us wants to be left out. At least our cable news tribes offer the common experience of getting to hate people together.

Design tactics. "Dark patterns" (to click this and not that) prompt users into actions that benefit the company but not necessarily the person.

Intrusive apps. Apps watch you in order to share reams of personal data based on your behavior.

Privacy concerns. Social media providers are invading users' privacy by manipulating newsfeeds to test their emotional state. Others are using artificial intelligence and machine learning on data gathered from voice-activated "personal assistants" and other accessories like watches—even tracking your medical health.

Smartphone distraction. Our phones hijack our minds. According to Apple, a typical smartphone owner pulls their phone out and uses it some eighty times a day, or nearly thirty thousand times over a year.

An interesting study by the *Journal of Computer-Mediated Communication* evaluated what happens when people can hear their phone ring but are unable to answer it. This situation caused spikes in blood pressure, faster pulse rates, and a decline in problem-solving skills.

Our smartphones have also threatened our sense of place. They allow us to escape from our real-life situations and connect with the unrealistic "highlight reels" others post to social media.

These moments of diversion and distraction add up, creating a near-permanent state of disengagement, which weakens the very fabric of our society.

Children-focused advertising. Children are viewed as a lucrative market, even though their brains are still developing. Businesses often see children (called "whales") as easy markets to mine profits because the technology is like oxygen to them.

- Red flags: When kids spend too much time on social media, video games, and other digital technology, parents see sleep problems, academic failure, social problems, anxiety and depression (due to upward social comparison), athletic kids giving up sports, and kids giving up social events or opportunities to do things outside the home because they want to stay in front of a screen.

- Video games: Gaming seeks a player's full engagement for as long as possible. Therefore, it affects the production of dopamine, a neurotransmitter tied to the brain's reward system and linked by research to addiction—keeping players engaged like a gambler chasing winning combinations on a slot machine.

Mental-health experts say the constant rewards the games provide can lead some players toward compulsive behavior.

- Kids see animated killing games that manage to be hair-raising without visible blood spilled.

- Using internet-linked, multiplayer games, kids today can play with total strangers.

- Studies also link gaming to poor behavior and lower school performance, along with the possible risk for increased substance use.

Use your authority and you will lose your influence . . .
Use your influence and you will gain authority.
–Loren Cunningham

Reflect to Connect

1. How has technology negatively impacted the lives of those around you?
2. What do you think about companies who target children with their addictive apps, games, and services?

Let's Get Off the Merry-Go-Round

If we as a country continue down this expedient path of irresponsibility, the rich will rule the poor with disdain in pursuit of greater riches, women and children will be exploited as the powerful rule the weak, and the young will extinguish the old in the name of convenience.

These are just some of the logical consequences of irresponsible and expedient thinking and behavior.

Remember the wisdom of The Freedom Paradox:

The more we behave irresponsibly, the more freedoms
we lose. The more we embrace responsibility, the greater
freedoms we enjoy.

The good news is that "We the People," as citizen-leaders, don't have to wait for our national leaders to change—we can begin changing ourselves.

Even in our own lives, unchecked emotions will always override intellect. And emotional decisions made in haste lead to poor outcomes.

I have observed that people who behave expediently pour so much energy and effort into their short-term emotions that they tend to lose sight of the long-term consequences.

Which is accurately described as a common version of insanity.

Insanity: doing the same thing over and over again but expecting different results.
–Anonymous

Would you like to get off the merry-go-round of expedience and set foot on solid ground? I have good news; you can stop going around in circles by changing how you think and making more principled decisions, which we'll cover in the next chapter.

One of the reasons people don't achieve their dreams is that they desire to change their results without changing their thinking.
–John Maxwell

Reflect to Connect

1. What have you experienced when you behave in an expedient way?
2. Do you keep doing the same thing, over and over, expecting different results?

CHAPTER SEVEN:

How to Make Better Decisions

Practicing Principled Behavior

> *It is in your moments of decision*
> *that your destiny is shaped.*
> **—Anthony Robbins**

To help you apply this principle to your own life, would you give me permission to ask you some questions?

If the weather is good, do you *feel* good? If it isn't, does it affect your attitude and your performance?

When people treat you well, do you *feel* well, and when people don't, do you become defensive or protective? Do your *emotions* change based on the behavior of others?

Are your *feelings* driven by circumstances, by your environment, by any kind of external conditions?

Do you *react* to changes and challenges by saying things like

- It's in my DNA. I inherited it from past generations.
- It's my parents' fault. I was raised that way.
- It's my boss's fault.
- It's my spouse's fault.
- It's the younger generation's fault.

- It's the government's fault.
- It's the economy.
- It's our society.

In other words, do you believe someone or something in your environment is responsible for your current situation, personal tendencies, or character? Do you feel increasingly victimized and out of control, not in charge of your life or your destiny?

> *Any time you think the problem is out there,*
> *that very thought is the problem.*
> **–Stephen R. Covey**

If you're not sure how to answer those questions, your words may provide a hint. Habitual language can be a strong indicator of whether you're reacting to your external situation and, therefore, allowing your feelings and emotions to dominate your response and absolve you of responsibility.

Take a look at the following chart and consider how often you use reactive language versus more responsible language.

Reactive Language	Underlying Belief	Responsible Alternative
"That's just the way I am."	There is nothing I can do about it.	"Let me look into my options."
"I can't do that."	Something outside me is limiting me.	"I am choosing not to do that."
"I just don't have time."	Something outside me is controlling my priorities.	"Let me see where I can schedule time into my calendar."

"My boss makes me so mad."	My emotional life is governed by someone outside my control.	"I need to ask my boss for some time to talk through this thing that frustrates me."
"I have to do it."	Circumstances or other people are forcing me to do it.	"I am choosing to do it."

The comments in the first column are evidence of a transfer of responsibility. Beneath these reactive comments is an expectation that someone or something else is responsible for our feelings and emotions. And as we give up our personal responsibility for our emotions, we empower other people, conditions, and circumstances to control us.

So, we blame; we use accusing attitudes and reactive, emotion-driven language; and we accrue increasing feelings of victimization for our own stagnant situation. The result is expedient decisions, which wreak havoc in our lives mentally, emotionally, spiritually, and physically.

Reflect to Connect

1. How do you react to changes and challenges?
2. When they occur, do you blame someone or something that is out of your control?

Principled Behavior Leads to Better Decisions

One thing I've learned about life is that your emotions, if left unchecked, will always override your intellect.

There was a time when I regularly met with some high school boys, and I would say to them, "When you get in the car with your buddies on Friday night, you already know how the night is going to turn out."

They knew what type of activities their friends might be involved in, and they knew the choices they would be faced with. So, I wanted them to understand that they needed to decide whether they were going out on the town Friday night *before* they were asked.

And if they chose to get in that car, they needed to decide *beforehand* how they were going to respond to the *emotional* situations that would occur that night.

> *Your unchecked emotions will always override your intellect.*

Like the proverbial frog in the pot, if we make decisions based on what "feels good at the moment" and simply "go with the flow," we will often wind up in hot water.

But if we make principled decisions based on what we know to be true and right, we'll experience less self-made trouble and greater success.

When you evaluate your behavior based on these two categories, you'll discover that virtually every action or decision you make can be described as either principled or expedient.

People who consistently say one thing but do something different choose to behave based on their emotions (in an expedient way) rather than on their *character* (in a principled way). People who behave expediently do what's *easiest* or what makes them the *happiest* in the *short run*. They find it more convenient to react to the urgent things in life. They are often guided by emotion and choose to make popular decisions that are rooted in unhealthy fears. At the same time, they worry about protecting their rights. Rash, emotional decisions lead to poor outcomes.

Those who are principled think about what is right in the long run and are self-disciplined to do it, even though it might not be the easiest, quickest, or most enjoyable thing to do.

They are proactive and focus on what is important, and they initiate action by filling their calendar with their *priorities* proactively, rather than being acted upon by other people's requests reactively.

Rather than jumping to what looks like a greener pasture on the other side, they first *invest* in fertilizing the pasture they are in currently.

They also choose to *trust* the process, which leads to principled decisions that are rooted in *faith*. At the same time, they accept their *responsibilities,* which accompany their rights.

When faced with situations that might test our *character*, we can use the following information by John Maxwell to help us reach **principled**, *character*-driven decisions.

Character-Driven People	Emotion-Driven People
Do right, then feel good	Feel good, then do right
Are commitment-driven	Are convenience-driven
Make principled decisions	Make popular decisions
Action controls attitude	Attitude controls action
Believe it, then see it	See it, then believe it
Create momentum	Wait for momentum
Ask, "What are my responsibilities?"	Ask, "What are my rights [freedoms]?"

Remember, character-driven people are willing to do things emotion-driven people will not bother to do. Character-driven people enjoy long-term success, while emotion-driven people usually wind up on the road to failure.

Reflect to Connect

1. Have you experienced the "boiling frog effect" in your own life?
2. Are you more character-driven or more emotion-driven in your decision-making?
3. Will you consider reviewing the chart above before you make your next big decision?

Four Strategies to Help You Make Better Decisions

Do you want to make better decisions? It's possible—*if* you focus on making character-driven decisions based on principles, instead of emotion-driven decisions based on expediency.

In chapter 1, I talked about the importance of "guarding your heart." Personally, I've learned it begins with looking into the mirror and admitting that the problem lies within me, that I need to take personal responsibility to lead me. I'm the only person who can change me.

When I consistently lead myself to make principled decisions, I avoid the consequences and results of expedient decisions.

And when I change me, I have learned that I inspire others to change, too, one step at a time—it is a process, a journey, and not a one-time event.

*He that can compose himself is wiser
than he that composes books.*
—Benjamin Franklin

The following is a four-pronged strategy to help you guard your heart. This strategy applies equally to all areas of life, regardless of whether you are on vacation with your family or negotiating a merger of billion-dollar companies.

It is easy to partition our lives into work, leisure, family, and other compartments, but your decisions must be consistently principled in *all* of these areas if you expect them to succeed and thrive.

Whether in the privacy of your home or in the seat of power in the corner office, your approach to making decisions will make or break you every time.

1. Protect Your Mind

My wife and I have three sons. They are all adults now, but I remember holding hands with them as we crossed the street when they were little boys.

Like most parents, we tried to protect them as best we could and help them avoid physical injury. Getting physically hurt would have been a tragedy, but there are other risks that are just as dangerous.

Fortunately, I discovered some ways to help us stay safe. From an early age, our boys have heard me talk about doing everything they can to protect their minds. I would say to them, "Your mind is like a computer . . . garbage in is garbage out. You want to protect what your eyes see and what your ears hear."

Those boys knew that I was going to ask them these questions:
- "What kind of music are you listening to?"
- "What movies do you plan to see?"
- "What TV shows are you watching?"

- "What videos are you observing?"
- "What websites are you visiting?"
- "What magazines/books/social media are you reading?"
- "What video games are you playing?"
- "What language do you and your friends use, and what jokes do you tell?"

I would share with them, "When you consistently allow enough garbage to come into your mind [in an expedient way], you will eventually begin to live out that same garbage, resulting in addiction and consequences."

I would continue, "On the other hand, when you more consistently protect what your eyes see and what your ears hear [in a principled way], you will live a life with growth, blessings, and success."

The same is true for all of us. Protecting our mind is the first step to making principled decisions.

I am who I am today because of
the choices I made yesterday.
–Eleanor Roosevelt

2. Change Your Thinking

We can better understand the importance of protecting our minds when we realize that everything begins with a *thought*.

A man is literally what he thinks, his character being the
complete sum of all his thoughts.
–James Allen

This can either be a good thing or a bad thing.

You can begin making principled, proactive, and character-driven decisions when you *change your thinking*. When you do, you will make an important discovery:

Unsuccessful people don't think like successful people do.

As you begin thinking for a change, it is important to understand these truths:

- You are responsible for your own choices, *and* you have the freedom to choose how you respond to what you experience in life.
- You can change (if you are willing and have the desire) how you *think* about making choices that lead to more right decisions.
- You can change where you spend your time and energy by focusing more on what you can control and less on what you cannot control.

One of the reasons people don't achieve their dreams is that they desire to change their *results* (in an expedient way) without changing their *thinking*. You can begin making principled decisions when you implement this "thinking for a change" process:

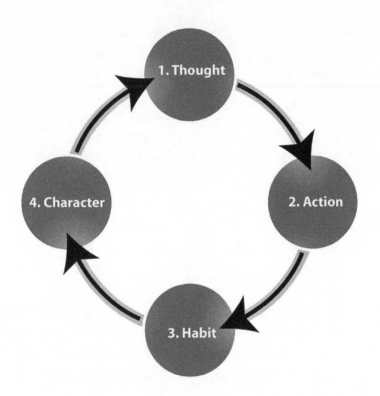

- Thought: Ponder what your eyes see and what your ears hear. Our thinking defines our direction and sets us up to take action.
- Action: Our action confirms our thinking and reflects our faith in our chosen path.
- Habit: It is said that if you act in a principled way for thirty to sixty days, you'll form a habit. Habits are the "autopilots" that guide our actions.
- Character: The things you routinely do will eventually define who you are. Your habits determine your character.

When you change what you think, you change what you do, and you change who you are.

3. Know Your Core Values and Purpose

Another key to making principled decisions is to evaluate opportunities in light of your core values and purpose. As we discussed in Part One, once we know and accept the core values and purpose of our nation, we can figure out our own specific core values and purpose.

Insight: I have learned that while your personal core values and purpose will be unique to you, they will not conflict with the core values and purpose of our nation.

Once I discovered my core values (who I am) and my purpose (why I exist) and wrote them down, it became easier to consistently make principled decisions—I made better decisions and made them faster.

When you know and live your changeless core values and life purpose, you can manage the warp-speed change going on all around you in every area of your life.

Why? Because you have created in your heart and mind a frame of reference, a set of principles by which you can *self-govern*—thereby living responsibly.

If you have not yet discovered your personal core values and purpose, I invite you to download the worksheets at TFP-book.com and schedule a time in your calendar to complete them.

4. Prepare a Plan

When you are faced with a choice between making a principled decision or an expedient one, you should:

- Pause, slow down, and breathe.
- Get in the habit of "sleeping on it" by waiting overnight before you make your final decision.
- Get wise counsel. If you are married, also ask your spouse.

- Create a T-chart and list the pros down one side of the paper and the cons on the other side.
- Ask questions and listen.

One of the best tools I have used to ask questions is the Rotary Club's guide for personal and professional relationships. It's called The Four-Way Test,[9] and it can be used to guide the things we think, say, and do:

1. Is it the *truth*?
2. Is it *fair* to all concerned?
3. Will it build *goodwill* and *better friendships*?
4. Will it be *beneficial* to all concerned?

When we protect our hearts and minds, change our thoughts, know our core values and purpose, and prepare a plan, we'll be positioned to make better decisions and make better decisions faster.

The ancestor of every action is a thought.
–Ralph Waldo Emerson

Reflect to Connect

1. What do you do to protect your heart and mind?
2. Are you willing to change your thinking in order to make better decisions? (Remember, changed thinking always precedes changed behavior.)

CHAPTER EIGHT:

Abundance versus Scarcity Mindsets

Your Perspective Determines Your Possibilities

*An abundance mindset always outperforms
a scarcity mindset in the long run.*

—Rory Vaden

George Washington's relentless nature colored everything he did, from riding his horse fast, even if he wasn't in a hurry, to holding his soldiers to high moral standards. His contagious leadership postured him with ironclad emotional control. According to a French envoy, he was even-tempered, tranquil, and orderly.

In victory and defeat, Washington maintained composure with a combination of seriousness, courage, tenacity, and outsized effort, which made teams stronger. Many officers marveled at how he inspired everyone to focus on the task and never appeared under distress.

When Washington pushed his troops to the limits of their endurance, he was always right beside them. In August 1776, during a risky attempt to evacuate nine thousand troops from Brooklyn, he manned the shore all night until the last boats had departed.

On Christmas Day, 1776, when he ordered a daring raid on a Hessian encampment across the icy and treacherous Delaware River, Washington's boat was the first to shove off. Over the course of the next ten days, his actions infected his ragtag army of outnumbered amateurs to defeat the Hessian mercenaries. Then came the Battle of Princeton in January 1777, where an opening barrage of musket volleys from the Redcoats sent the Continental Army into a panic, and its ranks began to splinter.

In a split-second decision, Washington burst to the front on a galloping white charger, riding high in the saddle under withering fire to circle and face his fearful troops, and he beseeched them to keep fighting. Then, according to one account, he reined in his horse and faced the enemy directly. This extraordinary effort compelled everyone to give more, and the victory over the Redcoats encouraged the Americans to believe that they could win the war.

In October 1777, after seeing more than one thousand colonial troops killed, wounded, or captured during a merciless rout at Germantown, Washington, even in defeat, sent the British commander a personal letter offering to return his dog, which had been found roaming the battlefield.[10]

So, how did Washington show such relentless, emotional fortitude in victory and defeat? He had an abundance mindset rather than a scarcity mindset.

Two Mindsets, Two Results

People with an abundance mindset believe that today's short-term pain, sacrifice, and investment in time, energy, and money will eventually bring long-term growth, blessings, and success.

People with an abundance mindset view their resources as a farmer views seeds. A successful farmer liberally sows seeds, trying to ensure a good fall harvest. He believes in the principle of sowing and reaping: the more he sows, the more he reaps.

Successful people with an abundance mindset see their resources as sufficient (plentiful) seeds to be sown. They know the harvest will come and more will be created.

Abundance thinkers believe there is always more where that came from.

-Michael Hyatt

In contrast, some people find it hard to invest resources because they feel so deficient. These people think with a *scarcity* mindset. Focused on expediency, they always feel that their commodities are about to run out.

You can't harvest if you haven't planted.

Consequently, people with a scarcity mindset tend to be protective of what they have and what they know. Their mindset encourages them to be selfish with their time, talent, and money.

If you have a *scarcity* mindset and never let go of what you have, you can never fully reach out for and grab hold of a greater opportunity of what could be.

Consider the differences between the abundance mindset and the scarcity mindset.

Abundance Mindset	Scarcity Mindset
Proactive	Reactive
Offensive	Defensive
Dynamic: Let's go!	Paralyzed: Hold on!
Pursue Vision	Prevent Loss
Create	Maintain
Think Win-Win	Think Win-Lose
Risk and Seize Opportunity	Guard and Protect Position

Bestselling author John Maxwell talks about the gap between two significant questions:

- "Can I?" is a question asked by those who have a scarcity mindset.
- "How can I?" is a question asked by those who have an abundance mindset.

People with a scarcity mindset think short-term and tend to exhibit *expedient* behavior, while people with an abundance mindset think long-term and tend to exhibit *principled* behavior. The more we understand the differences between an abundance mindset and a scarcity mindset, the more likely we'll be to make principled decisions from a place of *abundance*.

Reflect to Connect

1. Which question do you most often ask, "Can I?" or "How can I?"
2. Will you approach your next challenge or opportunity with the question, "How can I?"

Why Abundant Thinkers Succeed with Flying Colors

An abundance mindset results in abundant thinking. I've learned five truths about abundant thinkers:

1. Abundant thinkers are content with who they are, even though they may be different.
2. Abundant thinkers possess strong character qualities.
3. Abundant thinkers teach their children to behave in a principled way and model this in their own behavior.
4. Abundant thinkers use their gifts to benefit others and to protect others from those who use evil means and are self-centered.
5. Abundant thinkers have a *positive* mindset.

People with an abundance mindset believe that today's short-term pain, sacrifice, and investment in time, energy, and money will eventually bring long-term growth, blessings, and success.

It turns out that people who adopt an abundance mindset approach life, challenges, and opportunities in a principled manner that literally paves the way for them to succeed.

Examples of Abundance and Scarcity Mindsets in America

How we see our current circumstance is much more important than the actual situation itself. Our response to life's challenges and opportunities will either reflect a mindset of abundance or scarcity.

An Attitude of Gratitude

If emotions could be bottled and sold, gratitude might be a controlled substance. People who express an abundance of thankfulness can experience a happiness "high" that can last for a long time. In the workplace, employees feel better about themselves when their boss expresses more gratitude for their efforts, and they even desire to work harder.

Leaders who set out to build grateful cultures often start by thanking their employees. Building happy teams isn't just a top-down job. Friendliness and gratitude also flow in many directions at once—from leaders to followers, followers to leaders, colleagues to colleagues, and even employees to customers and suppliers.

In today's selfie culture, which often rewards bragging and arrogance over kindness and humility, studies have found that gratitude was associated with greater well-being. Grateful people experience daily hassles and annoyances just like everyone else, but they tend to view setbacks through a different lens, reframing challenges in a positive light.

Try to be a rainbow in someone's cloud.
–Maya Angelou

Children who rate higher in gratitude tend to be happier and more engaged at school, as compared with their less grateful peers, and to give and receive more social support from family and friends. They also tend to experience fewer depressive symptoms and less anxiety, and they are less likely to exhibit antisocial behavior, such as aggression.

Students who were more grateful were also better at managing their lives and identifying important goals for the future. They enjoyed stronger relationships with their peers because their positive disposition made them more attractive and likable. They were perceived by peers as having a warmer personality and being more friendly and thoughtful.

For parents, a good way to encourage gratefulness is simply to set a better example (e.g., express thanks or gratitude daily to their spouse).

It's also important for children and adults to notice and acknowledge the larger circle of people who benefit their lives, like the school secretary or janitor.

Reflect to Connect

1. Who can you express gratitude to this week?
2. What can you do today to improve your own spirit of gratefulness?

Those who don't live with a perspective of gratitude gravitate to a mindset of scarcity. They let emotions, especially fear, rule their thinking and behavior. As a result, their potential, happiness, and impact on others is limited. We can see this in the following examples.

Protecting Popular Programs

Instead of considering every option of change in order to survive and even thrive as a nation (while preserving our core values and purpose), people in our country are driven by fear and emotion to protect their popular entitlement programs, such as social security, agriculture, welfare, and individual and corporate tax incentives.

Entitlement programs. Not only are the people of our country behaving with a scarcity mindset but our country's leaders and even employees of our government are also driven by fear. They fear losing their power and position (their jobs) and choose to protect them at all costs. Why do you think our country's leaders tend to "over promise and under deliver" when it comes to making needed changes to these entitlement programs?

Special tax treatment. When big business uses its influence with our country's leaders for special tax treatments or supports laws and regulations to protect their market position or market share, the people of our country lose. Our standard of living and quality of life suffer because creative, innovative, and less expensive products and services are stifled by the protective position of big business.

Political Donations

Responsibility is lacking (in both directions) between the leaders of our country and special political forces when our country's leaders accept large donations (though legal) with a "wink and nod." The same issue is exemplified in the "pay to play" attitude of political special interest groups, lobbyists, and super PACs.

What happened to the credibility and accountability of our political system that was guided by the truth and the interests of John and Jane Doe on Main Street? When the people see their national leaders behave this way, they begin to model the same scarcity mindset.

Reflect to Connect

1. What examples of scarcity thinking can you see in our government?
2. What can you do to help others see the negative impact of a scarcity mindset?

How to Develop an Abundance Mindset

Do you have an abundance mindset or scarcity mindset?

Here's another way to ask that question: how do you see your glass—half full or half empty? I have observed that people who see their glass as half empty have a scarcity mindset. And once you see your glass as half empty, it's like wearing a blindfold that limits your ability to see where you are going.

People who see their glass as half full have an abundance mindset. They open their minds to see where they are going (their vision), and help the most people along the way.

I'm one of those people who has always seen my glass as half *full* because I believe that more is always coming to fill my glass, until it overflows.

When I look over my life, I don't have any regrets. Have I made mistakes? Yes. Have I had times when I was very disappointed? Yes. Still, somehow, I have always learned from my mistakes, overcome disappointments, and moved forward. Even when I make a mistake, instead of dwelling on it, my thinking usually goes to considering my next options.

Over time, I have realized that my perspective comes from principled decisions supported by an abundance mindset and a grateful heart.

Every person can develop an abundance mindset by adopting the following five attributes.

1. Understand There Is Enough for Everyone

Abundant thinkers know there is enough in the world for everyone to share in a piece of the pie. They understand that the more you share in a principled way, the more the abundance grows.

Scarcity thinkers believe there is not enough of anything to go around. They fear that there will not be enough for them, especially if they share with others.

2. Give Time, Talent, and Treasures

Abundant thinkers know that giving their time, talent, and treasures will come back to them in so many ways, thus increasing *the abundance in* their own lives. This *principled* process strengthens and fosters team-building and creative thinking that supports continual improvement.

Scarcity thinkers do *not* share. After all, they are driven by a deep-seated belief (in an *expedient* way) that there isn't enough to go around, so they cannot afford to give anything away. They truly believe that if they share their knowledge or wealth, they will lose power and possessions both now and in the future.

The freedom and success enjoyed by abundant thinkers becomes obvious when we contrast it with the limiting beliefs of scarcity thinkers.

Scarcity thinking weakens our effectiveness and keeps us from realizing our full potential. But a perspective of abundance ensures that there's always enough to go around and keeps us moving forward.

When I was in high school and in college, I always did the extra credit work. I didn't need the extra grade because I usually already had an *A* in the class. So, why?

When my dad suddenly died and I became the boss of our family company at twenty years old, I would stay up late into the night diligently studying about our industry, as well as trends in other industries. Why?

Somehow, I just knew that through all this extra effort, I was developing and building my character—who I was becoming. I approached life with an abundance mindset, and I knew that, personally, I had so much more room to grow.

3. Don't Compare Yourself with Others

Abundant thinkers don't compare themselves with others—only with themselves. They set realistic goals and then work to achieve them. They encourage others to do the same. Their goals are based (in a principled way) upon a logical study of achievable results in each step.

Scarcity thinkers continually ask themselves why they aren't like others or why they do not have the things others have. They often view others as younger, prettier, or more handsome, and they conclude that such characteristics give those others unique advantages.

Scarcity thinkers focus on the outcomes and achievements of successful people and fail to acknowledge the investment of time, money, and resources that always precedes such success.

4. Think Win-Win

Abundant thinkers find common ground with their colleagues and fellow citizens. They know that unresolved conflict is wasted time and energy and subtracts from an abundant environment.

They see the possibility of *win-win* and assume that there is a way for all concerned to profit and thrive. They understand that constructive criticism (offered in a principled way) helps others to grow.

Scarcity thinkers want to be at the center of attention because they want all they can get for themselves. They know (sometimes unconsciously) that for this to happen, others have to lose. They think that if they can use expedient means to get something done more quickly, their "win" justifies their "survival of the fittest" approach.

5. Embrace Gratitude

Abundant thinkers live lives of *gratitude* for the abundance of the world in which they live. They are positive and upbeat. To them, life is a continuously replenished bowl of fresh fruit—all ripe for the taking. They teach others how to be positive and live in gratitude.

Scarcity thinkers are *not* grateful for what they have. They see their life's accomplishments as the result of only their own hard work and are unable to give heartfelt thanks to others for helping.

The more we understand the differences between an abundance mindset and a scarcity mindset, the more likely we'll be able to make principled decisions from a place of abundance—and our nation will experience more abundance as well.

Reflect to Connect

1. Do you have an abundance mindset or a scarcity mindset?
2. What challenge or opportunity are you facing today that would benefit from a shift toward an abundance mindset?

CHAPTER NINE:

Symptoms versus Root Cause

When Is the Problem Really the Problem?

We often preoccupy ourselves with the symptoms, whereas if we went to the root cause of the problems, we would be able to overcome the problems once and for all.

—Wangari Maathai

After the French and Indian War, Great Britain had control of more land on the American continent than any other European country. But the small island nation did not have the capacity to manage the massive resources it had just won.

With forest, farmland, new ports, and mineral treasures in Canada and down the Mississippi River valley, Great Britain had many ways to offset the costs of defending its colony.

But George III and his Parliament decided on the easiest way. They would limit their expenses by prohibiting development of the new lands and making the American colonists pay for their own defense.

A series of confiscatory taxes created bad blood between these former comrades in arms; after all, American colonists had just fought beside their British cousins in the recent war.

But when Americans protested the taxes and acted to prevent them, Great Britain sent more troops, forced the Americans to house and feed them, and ignored the many reasonable petitions for representation and rights as British citizens.

Both sides, for a time, danced around a fundamental disagreement about who Americans were and what the crown owed them. Americans saw themselves as British citizens who had a right to elect the local officials that governed them and to pay a reasonable amount for mutual defense and infrastructure.

Americans owed loyalty to the king, not to Parliament. Meanwhile, the king and Parliament saw American colonists on the order of something less than citizens, people who owed money to the crown but were owed no say in their own governing in return.

The king and Parliament treated the symptoms of this disagreement by issuing harsher and harsher laws and acts that treated the colonists not like subjects but like slaves.

Colonists, like John and Samuel Adams, John Hancock, Joseph Warren, and Paul Revere, saw that Britain would not address the root cause of the trouble. So, they set about to address it themselves.

They dumped tea into Boston Harbor to protest the tax on it. They forced British judges out of court and set up their own courts to judge each other fairly. They set up Committees of Correspondence to spread information quickly and independently.

And they established the famous Minute Men to ensure that they could raise a defense quickly in case of threat. They saw what they would need to do to secure their own freedom, and they did it. Before the first shot was ever fired, these Massachusetts men acted in the liberty they later declared and fought to win formally.

Stand your ground. Don't fire unless fired upon, but if they mean to have war, let it begin here.

–Captain John Parker to the Minutemen, April 19, 1775

Unlike the Massachusetts colonists, people in other colonies kept writing to Britain, hoping to address the symptoms of mistreatment. John Dickinson of Delaware wrote the Olive Branch Petition asking the king to change specific actions toward the colonists.

Letters flew back and forth over the Atlantic addressing British wrongs and asking for reconsideration, for change, for justice. But none of those pleas for reason found an answer in action.

When the Massachusetts colonists knew that force was the only avenue left for them, the Adams cousins, Hancock, Warren, Revere, and others organized raids on British munitions and raised a standing army.

After the first formal engagement at Lexington and Concord, they made sure to fight the propaganda war effectively by rushing their own accounts of British treachery and violence to London ahead of the British military reports.

Massachusetts drew a line in the sand that the other colonies could not long ignore. They went straight to the root cause of the problem between Parliament and the colonies and acted.[11]

Reflect to Connect

1. How did the actions of those from Massachusetts differ from the actions from the other colonists?
2. Do you sometimes focus on the symptoms rather than addressing the root cause of your problems?

Identifying Cause and Effect

In 1666, as the story goes, Sir Isaac Newton sat in a garden and came up with the Law of Gravity after watching an apple fall to the ground (or after it hit him on the head, depending on which version you believe).

The principle suggested by this law is easy enough to understand: when gravity pulls, the apple drops.

> *Shallow men believe in luck.*
> *Strong men believe in cause and effect.*
> **–Ralph Waldo Emerson**

In a cause and effect relationship, one action or event (the cause) makes another event happen (the effect). One cause could have several effects.

- The cause is *why* it happens. To determine a cause, ask, "Why did this happen?"
- The effect is *what* happens. To identify an effect, ask, "What happened?"

There are four criteria that can help us understand this important principle:

1. The cause has to occur before the effect.
2. Whenever the cause happens, the effect must also occur.
3. The strength of the cause also determines the strength of the effect.
4. The effect is actually due to the cause rather than to some other event or cause.

What are some examples of cause and effect?
Cause: Jump in the pool.

Effect: Get wet.

Cause: Your gas tank is empty.
Effect: Your car won't start.

Cause: In business, you don't submit invoices in a timely manner.
Effect: Your payment comes later than you expected.

Reflect to Connect

1. Can you think of other examples of cause and effect?
2. How do you usually identify what is a cause and what is an effect?

Distinguishing Symptoms from the Root Cause

When you're resolving a problem, it's important to understand the difference between cause and effect—between a *symptom* and the *root cause.*

- A symptom is an indicator or sign that a problem exists.
- A root cause is the fundamental reason for, or source of, the problem.

It's not always easy to sift through the chaos of a situation—particularly one that's gone off the rails—and determine the contributing factors that brought you to where you are. At first glance, we often make snap decisions based on a shallow, expedient evaluation of the situation. See the following illustration. Which central dark circle looks larger?

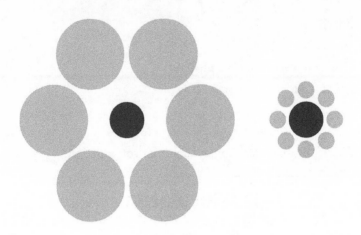

Most people answer that the right circle is larger. A more careful evaluation of the image reveals the truth that the left and right dark circles are the same size. Your perception is influenced by the size of the surrounding grey circles.

Symptoms can often appear like they are the root cause to the problem. This is why it's so important to take a deep breath, step back, and evaluate the particulars of the concern. When needed, dig deeper until you discover the root cause.

Solving this mystery can be challenging. And often, we are distracted by the mere symptoms of our problem.

Root Cause Analysis

One way to discover the root cause of a problem is to perform a simple *root cause analysis*. A root cause analysis just requires you to ask a series of *why* questions.

For example, if employees in the workplace have low morale, it is a sign of a problem. Low morale doesn't happen by itself, and it can't be resolved by itself.

If you were the leader, you may ask, "Why do my employees have low morale?" The answer might be that they are fearful and lack trust in management. If you ask, "Why are my employees afraid and lack trust?" The answer may be that you have a manager who exhibits destructive behavior. Next, you ask, "Why does my manager exhibit destructive behavior?" and so on.

Each time you can answer the *why* question, you have probably identified a symptom that is actually caused by something else. So, continue to ask *why* for each answer until you can no longer generate a logical response. You now have likely reached the root cause that has generated the observed symptoms.

Tip: Once you think you've asked your last "why" question, try to ask "why" one more time. Often, we need to really push through to the end of this process to arrive at the genuine root cause of our problem.

When you have identified the *root cause*, put an action plan in place to solve the problem—which prevents future reoccurring problems. Amazingly, many of the *symptoms* will go away as well.

Notice that if you take action too early in the process, you wind up merely addressing the symptoms (often ineffectively).

Imagine our scenario mentioned above (employees with low morale). If you immediately launched a cheery, "Let's get positive!" campaign with your people, you would have missed the root cause of the morale problem altogether.

Reflect to Connect

1. Have you ever performed a root cause analysis on a particular issue or problem?
2. Will you try asking "why" multiple times as you tackle your next problem?

Distinguishing Needs and Wants

Another important principle related to symptoms and root cause is distinguishing *needs* from *wants*. The greatest gap in the world is understanding the difference between what you "want" (symptom) and what you "need" (root cause).

Everyone can achieve what they have always wanted by changing how they think about what they need.

The following chart details the differences between needs and wants.

Needs	Wants
A requirement that must be fulfilled in order to survive, an essential	Something you wish to have, nonessential, often based on emotions
Based on principles that do not change with time	Based on assumptions that can change over time
If unfulfilled, "We the People" will suffer	If unfulfilled, "We the People" will continue in the same direction
"We the People" all have the same needs	"We the People" have different wants

Needs and wants are separate forces that compel action for satisfaction. Needs are principles that, if not met on time, put the survival of our nation at stake. In contrast, wants are something people crave; they are popular, provide immediate self-gratification, and/or make you feel good in the short term, but unsatisfied wants do not challenge our nation's survival.

Needs can be distinguished from wants based on their level of importance. Needs, which address a root cause, are of the utmost importance. However, people will often contend that their wants, which are desires based on symptoms, are of immense importance, even though they may or may not be realistically able to obtain them.

Reflect to Connect

1. Do you find it difficult to distinguish between needs and wants?
2. Think about the products and services you have used today. Which are needs? Which are wants?

Examples of Focusing on Symptoms in America

Distinguishing symptoms from the root cause helps us focus on the real problem. Many people, however, focus on the "problem" that is most obvious, which is often just a symptom.

American Politics

Let's first look at how most of our country's leaders offer an expedient way to solve our symptoms (our perceived problems) without searching for the root cause.

- **Crime.** When crime increases in a city, we hire more and more police officers and purchase more military equipment for dealing with the crime.
- **Violence.** When violence increases, we pass more and more criminal laws to convict the offenders. Then we build more prisons for them.
- **Drug addiction.** When drug addiction increases, we build more and more drug rehab facilities.
- **Obesity.** When people continue to gain unhealthy weight, we tax sugary beverages.

- **Other problems.** When our country is faced with issues and problems, our country's leaders tend to produce policies and cast more laws and regulations upon us (a symptom). However, the laws and regulations do not inspire people to change their behavior.

Since laws and regulations do not inspire us to greatness, excellence, or virtue, our issues and problems continue to exist. Then our leaders produce and cast even more laws and regulations upon us, and the cycle repeats. This is what I call the "doom loop."

Reflect to Connect

1. Do you agree that laws and regulations do not inspire us to greatness?
2. Can you identify the root cause for one of the symptoms listed above?

Often our national, state, and local leaders expediently cave in and address short-term, feel-good wants, which are symptoms. They fail to identify the long-term need or root cause because they do not go deeper and use a root cause analysis.

Political Promises

Let's now examine another symptom found in American politics. Often, many leaders during an election campaign lure "We the People" (like a fisherman lures a fish with bait on a hook) by offering to solve our perceived problems (symptoms) so they can "hook" us to vote for them. Why?

We are emotionally attracted to (in an expedient way) and crave those who make these unrealistic claims in hopes we'll transfer our responsibility to them. Then they underdeliver (on what we need—the root cause) on their overpromised claims. Why?

Because too many elected leaders are like "snake oil salesmen" who are only interested in themselves, focusing on *me* and not *we* to gain more power, position, and possessions for themselves.

Then when they underdeliver on their promises, they tell "We the People" that something or someone outside them (an expedient excuse) kept them from solving our problems.

> *Never ruin an apology with an excuse.*
> **–Ben Franklin**

Next, they say that we need to re-elect them so they can go back to solving our perceived problem. Today, voters are frustrated because our government has become big and polarized, and our political leaders are out of touch, out of reach, and out of sync with those they represent.

> *If you kick the can down the road on verification,*
> *then you can have trouble because you are going*
> *to eventually trip over that can.*
> **–Robert Gallucci**

There is growing suspicion, even disdain, for elites and institutions that seem removed from the daily lives of ordinary people, and many Americans feel disconnected from their own government.

If Americans feel that they're losing control of their future, they will push back. That is why people feel America is guided more by government than the governed. However, ordinary people are perfectly capable of making complicated policy choices.

You could ask, "What would it take to reimagine democracy so that the will of the people is meaningful and consequential?" Treat Americans as participants in the decision-making process instead of our current approach of treating Americans as only fans—telling "We the People" only after a decision has been made.

Often, Americans, if asked, could help make a better decision because "We the People" are the ones impacted by that decision and asked to carry out those decisions.

Today with technology (e.g., video conference calling), Americans can be reached in the most remote corners of the planet to engage in dialogue and offer feedback.

Reflect to Connect

1. Have you ever felt that an elected official failed to deliver what he or she promised?
2. What do you think about being a participant in American democracy, instead of just a bystander?

Let's now look at the three most important societal institutions of the family—home, school, and church—to identify some of the most glaring symptoms that indicate far deeper root causes.

American Families

Many parents are focused on how they are perceived as parents, rather than the long-term well-being and maturity of their children.

They are more concerned about external appearance than the internal character of their children. They focus on the outcome or results their children achieve (e.g., becoming the soccer team captain, going to an elite universality, attaining a successful career, or achieving wealth). They place little or no value on helping their children become responsible citizens of our country. They fail to build character internally so their children can handle the external, changing conditions that are coming at them at warp speed.

Prepare the child for the path, not the path for the child.
–Betsy Brown Braun

What happens on the inside (*how* the child is maturing) will have far more influence on the child's future life than the external *things* that tend to consume the parents' energy and emotions. Ironically, often, the struggles presented by difficulties forge the finest character qualities.

Let's look at three types of parents who are driven for results—mainly because their children have become the parent's brand. If their child succeeds, they are successful parents. If they are successful parents, their status is enhanced, and everyone respects successful parents. However, the kids pick up cues that the main purpose of an education is to just "look good."

These self-serving motivations are the reason why we've recently witnessed these scenarios:

- We have heard about the college admissions scandal where parents cheated and bribed to get their kids admitted to elite universities. This occurred even though studies have shown that there is a strong connection between how engaged a student is in and out of college classes and their future job satisfaction and well-being—what students *do* at college seems to matter much more than where they *go*.
- We have seen wealthy parents transfer legal guardianship of their college-bound children to relatives or friends so their child can claim financial aid scholarships and access to federal financial aid designed for the poor.

Snowplow parenting. Well-meaning parents, who believe their task is primarily to prepare the way or path for their children, eliminate obstacles, smooth out the rough places, and generally make life a painless, trouble-free experience for their children.

These parents miss out on preparing their child to behave in a principled way for the many twists and turns life will present.

When parents organize their lives around their kids, those kids expect everyone else to as well. This leads to an entitlement mentality, and when children are raised to feel entitled to everything, they feel grateful for nothing.

Helicopter parenting. Out of care and concern and good intentions, these parents are always rescuing their kids.

Protective and micromanaged parenting is evident in children who ride in car seats until they are in middle school and bounce on soft-surface playgrounds. These kids rarely walk home from school on their own, ride their bicycles around neighborhoods, or go on errands for their parents.

Children hear the world is an inherently dangerous place because social interaction carries the risk of being hurt. Their lives are so structured and analytical that they lack opportunity for independence and decision-making.

Their lives are rigidly structured, which leads to a decline in unfettered play and saps creativity and imagination. If you took ten kids to a pond today and said, go play, they would say, "What do we do?"

Parents are demanding privileges for their children that have little to do with educational progress. They ask for report-card mercy when their child can't make the grade. Parents are expecting more from our teachers while shouldering less responsibility at home.

Perfectionist parenting. Many parents set a high bar for achievement, but some push for even more; they ask for near perfection. Their kids' lives are organized around building the perfect college application by securing the best grades, test scores, and extracurricular activities.

Unlike hardworking people, who enjoy striving for lofty goals and cope well with setbacks, perfectionists aim for high standards in order to demonstrate their worth to others, and then, they are brutally critical of themselves when they fall short. Today, parents feel responsible for their children's achievements and deeply internalize their children's failures.

It's like chasing a carrot that you never actually catch because what you achieve is never enough. There is always something more—better grades, bigger promotions, or higher salaries—which leaves you feeling that who you are is never enough.

Some children adopt perfectionist thinking and behavior by imitating the perfectionism their parents display. Parents withhold praise for a less-than-perfect performance on a report card. Children internalize the belief that they won't be loved unless they meet their parents' unrealistic and rigid standards—which sometimes leads to cheating.

Perfectionism can lead to serious mental health issues, including anxiety, loneliness, depression, eating disorders, and even suicidal thoughts, as well as impulsivity and risky behaviors, such as sex and substance abuse.

Colleges and employers are finding more and more students and young employees with anxiety and other mental-health issues, leading students and young employees to withdraw, turn negative, and overreact to stress.

Poor sportsmanship. Many years ago, you only heard "trash talk" in professional sports. In recent years, we've seen occasional outbursts of unsportsmanlike conduct by parents at kids' games—mainly over the officiating.

Now, you find kids in sports using "trash talk" (even profanity) toward the opposing team's members. Even more distressing, you can observe coaches and parents on the sidelines and in the bleachers yelling and complaining all nine innings, or four quarters, or two halves. This conduct makes life on the field or in the bleachers miserable.

Twenty years from now, none of those kids will remember the score of that game. But they will remember adults acting like children and the embarrassment they felt at their parents' words. Any adult who thinks such behavior is about being competitive knows nothing about competing and even less about why children show up to play.

Parents and coaches, it is time to step up to the plate and set the appropriate and responsible example.

Reflect to Connect

1. Do you know any Snowplow or Helicopter parents? How about perfectionist parents? How do these parents impede the development of their children?
2. Have you witnessed any child-like, emotional behavior by parents on the sidelines at sporting events?
3. What do you think is the root cause of these dysfunctional forms of parenting?

American Schools

Now let's look at our schools. Have you noticed any of the following?

- **Scores over scholarship.** Classroom behavior issues are directly related to the absence of principled parents in the home. Also, the emphasis in our schools has shifted to a near-singular focus on passing the standardized tests required to advance to the next grade. Teachers are expected to teach how to correctly answer the test questions and have little time left to teach critical thinking and how to think more deeply by asking quality questions.

- **Competence over character.** At an accelerated pace, our schools have moved to teach only job skills and competence over character qualities, like responsibility or teamwork. These principled "soft" skills are exactly what employers are desperately seeking.

- **Career over civics.** Our schools have seen a steep decline in the teaching of civics in favor of more career-oriented classes.

American Churches

We even see symptom-centric behavior in our churches. Sadly, many churches are experiencing a decline in attendance. Often such decline is a result of church leaders who (in an expedient way) sought culture-based solutions without regard to the life principles revealed in the Bible. Therefore, people see church attendance and participation as irrelevant.

So, if all of the above are symptoms, what is the root cause? The root cause to our country's issues and problems in our culture is that individual rights (freedoms) are no longer anchored to personal responsibility. Therefore, we've sabotaged our ability to self-govern.

Addressing Root Causes Takes Time

We've established that changes in our cultural thinking and behavior have all but eliminated our practice of principled responsibility. The burning question is, "What can we do to turn the tide of despair and progress toward a better future that once again incorporates responsibility into our national culture?"

As we attempt to answer that question for ourselves and as a society, we should acknowledge that it has taken us generations to get to where we are today, and the problems will not be solved overnight.

When you solve *symptoms,* you are only making the pain go away for a short while, but you have not addressed the *root cause.*

When you have identified the *root cause*, you can put an action plan in place to solve the problem. And amazingly, many of the *symptoms* will go away as well.

Reflect to Connect

1. Have you noticed the shift from critical thinking to test scores in your children's schools?
2. In your local schools, have you seen an emphasis on competence with little or no attention directed to students' character?
3. Have churches in your community changed so much that they risk the preservation of their core values and beliefs?

CHAPTER TEN:

Process and Content

What We Say and Do, and How We Say and Do It

*To lead yourself, use your head; to lead others,
use your heart. Always touch a person's heart before
you ask him for a hand.*

—John Maxwell

In the summer of 1775, the Second Continental Congress convened in Philadelphia. Though members of the Congress would not sign the Declaration of Independence for another year, the colonies were already engaged in a difficult and bloody war against the most powerful military in the world, Great Britain.

But they were determined to stand up for their God-given rights.

With violence escalating and the war becoming even more gruesome, Congress commissioned George Washington as commander-in-chief of the Continental Army. Less than a month after taking charge, Washington made one of his first requests, something he knew would be a vital and necessary component for his military operation.

As a military commander, Washington anticipated the toll war would take on his troops, especially knowing the incredible effort on the part of the colonists to defeat a formal standing army.

Of course, he knew how important it was for his soldiers to be physically prepared, but he also understood that he would need something more in the face of such odds—spiritual fortitude and the moral strength to persevere.

Though many ministers were already volunteering alongside colonial troops, Washington wanted their services recognized and financially compensated; he wanted them to become an official part of the army.

On July 29, 1775, Congress granted Washington's request, and the Army Chaplain Corps was born. There would be one chaplain for each regiment in the Continental Army. Receiving a captain's pay, they would attend to the spiritual, emotional, and even physical wellbeing of the troops.

Since the inception of the Corps, chaplains have served in every American war. Older even than the United States, the Chaplain Corps was, and is today, integral to the fabric of our nation and instrumental to our military's success.[12]

Washington's first request demonstrated a priority in his new leadership role. As the commander-in-chief, his focus was on people, caring for his troops, as well as things, enhancing *relationships*, as he drove for the *results* of winning the war. He clearly understood that he needed what I call *process* (*how* you say and do) *and content* (*what* you say and do).

> *Rather than focusing on results, focus on investing in the people who will get you those results.*

In contrast, let's take a look at another leader whose sole focus was only on *content* (*what* he wanted to say and do)—with complete disregard for *process* (*how* he said and did it)—and on *results* to the exclusion of *relationships*.

In 1899, a largely unknown Communist agitator named Vladimir Lenin composed his first major writing, *The Development of Capitalism in Russia*. The book was a success, despite the fact that Lenin had no training in economics and Russia had an agrarian, not a capitalist, economy at the time. For nearly two decades, Lenin continued to write. Though he was born to a middle-class family, he cast himself as the hero of the working class. Despite the fact that he had never marched in the streets or been in any real confrontation, he incited others to violent opposition of the government.

He viewed the pen as an instrument of war and urged his readers to arm themselves with revolvers, bombs, knives, and rags soaked in kerosene to beat up and kill their rivals.

Lenin dealt brutally with his detractors in print also, practicing a kind of scorched-earth journalism. One historian described his literary style this way: "Intolerant, sarcastic, correct about everything, and hell-bent on having the last word, Lenin was a master troll, king of the flame war."[13]

Lenin wanted to recreate the world according to his vision. The tools of his trade were alternative facts, incendiary provocation, mocking, derision, sarcasm, and arguments that had no basis in logic or reality. And he succeeded.

On October 25, 1917, Bolshevik forces began the Communist Revolution in Russia, which put Lenin's violent language into flesh-and-blood terms.

More than four hundred thousand were killed in the civil war, and as many as seventy to one hundred million more died as a series of Communist dictators translated Lenin's incendiary rhetoric into action. Every word has power. A leader's words have even greater power.

George Washington and Vladimir Lenin had two very different approaches when they made decisions, outlined plans, or conveyed instructions. Washington understood that there were two key factors involved: process *and* content, relationships *and* results.

However, Lenin believed there was only one factor involved: content, or results. Lenin believed that the process (the how) did not matter as long as you obtained the results (the what). The ends always justify the means.

> *A lie told often enough becomes the truth.*
> **–Vladimir Lenin**

Washington understood something that Lenin never did:

> *The more we behave irresponsibly, the more freedoms we lose. The more we embrace responsibility, the greater freedoms we enjoy. (The Freedom Paradox)*

Like principled versus expedient behavior, the issue of process *and* content is a significant one for our culture. In this chapter, we will explore the principle of process *and* content, and how our culture has slowly drifted from Washington's responsible approach of building success to Lenin's irresponsible, destructive approach to obtain power. In the next chapter, we'll explore how we can shift toward prioritizing both process and content in our own lives.

Process *and* Content

Let's look more deeply at these two key factors. One is the *content*, or what has to be decided. The other is the *process* whereby the decision is made.

Content

Technically, *content* is defined as "the amount of something in a container." Content is usually measurable and quantifiable. In the context of our life and work, when content is our main concern, we

- Drive for *results*.
- Focus on *things*.
- *Manage* things.
- Concentrate on *what* we say and do.

With content, the focus is on *what* the final results are. Content always comes before process.

Content is very important. Without clear, well-communicated, meaningful, and attainable objectives, people are directionless. The people need to know *what* you expect.

Process

Process, on the other hand, is commonly defined as "a series of actions directed toward a specific aim." Process involves *how* we interact with people and *how* we communicate with them. With process, the focus is on people: influencing and leading them, enhancing relationships, and intentionally monitoring *how* we say or do things.

Process is just as important as content. Working well with others enables you to bring out the very best in people, for people, and through people.

There are two important aspects to process:

- **How we say it**. Here we focus on how we communicate and interact with people on a day-to-day basis. **How** we say something can significantly impact what the recipient of the message feels is being conveyed. Our body language and tone of voice can reinforce or contradict the message in the words we are saying.

- **How we do it**. Here we focus on how we interact with people to set and pursue our goals. For example, the way we define an objective would be the process side of a task.

Embrace the how as you pursue the what.

Reflect to Connect

1. How would you define "content"?
2. How would you define "process"?
3. Do you think more about *what* you do (content) or *how* you do it (process)?

The Principle That Can Transform You

We need both process *and* content. Bestselling author Jim Collins, in his book *Built to Last*, said, "Instead of being oppressed by the 'Tyranny of the OR,' highly visionary companies liberate themselves with the 'Genius of the AND' . . . Instead of choosing between A OR B, they figure out a way to have both A AND B."

Collins went on to say that this was *not* about "balance," in which you go to the midpoint, fifty-fifty or half and half. Instead, it's about accomplishing both at the same time, all the time.

People who embrace the principle of content and process understand the genius of the "and." They don't limit themselves to one solution or approach to a problem or challenge. Rather, they embrace two seemingly incompatible truths simultaneously.

How you say or do something can make or break
what you've said or done.
–Jim Lundy

Process and content are often expressed using different words. Let's take another look at a list that matches expressions for **process** with corresponding expressions for **content.**

Process	Content
We enhance *relationships*.	We drive for *results*.
The focus is on *people*.	The focus is on *things*.
We lead *people*.	We manage *things*.
The focus is on *how* we say and do.	The focus is on *what* we say and do.

Although people use different words in different contexts, the principle of process and content appear in almost every aspect of our life.

If you're like most people, you tend toward content, not process. You like to focus on the task at hand, make decisions, and "get 'er done." But we must focus on both to achieve maximum effectiveness.

If you don't take time to work on your communication on the process side, you'll spend a whole lot more time down the road trying to repair the damage done by barking expedient statements.

How can we apply what we have learned?

If you start to look for it, you'll see the potential to use this powerful duo of process and content in every area of your life. As you begin to learn and apply this principle, it will literally transform the way you think, speak, and behave.

Reflect to Connect

1. Do you naturally focus more on content or process?
2. Will you embrace the "how" as you pursue the "what"?

Relationships *and* Results

Let's focus on one area where process and content often shows up: the issue of relationships versus results. Over the years, I have learned that the most effective people never lose sight of the fundamental importance of driving for results. They need to be good at analyzing, planning, prioritizing, deciding, initiating, and following through on commitments.

So, if we need to focus on results, should we do so at the expense of relationships? No, I have learned that it is not an either-or situation. Focusing on both relationships *and* results multiplies your effectiveness.

Let me show you what I mean. I coined the term *Effectiveness Quotient* to describe or rate a person's level of effectiveness, following this both/and way of thinking.

To determine a leader's Effectiveness Quotient, you would first rate a person's focus and drive as they relate to results on a scale from one to ten. Then you would rate the person's focus and intention related to building and maintaining relationships, also on a scale from one to ten.

This person's Effectiveness Quotient would be the results rating times the relationship rating. So, a person with a results rating of six and a relationship rating of three would have an Effectiveness Quotient of eighteen.

I have found that it's not unusual for people to rate pretty well on results and fairly low on relationships.

Effectiveness Quotient

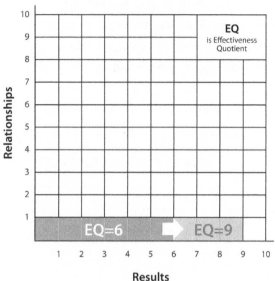

Results

Look at the lower-left rectangle on the graph above. It represents the effectiveness of someone who reaches a six on the results scale (about average) and a one on the relationship scale (very low).

This person would focus on the bottom line and the end results of his work. Also, it's fair to say that he probably doesn't care much about building and enhancing relationships.

Even for those whose effectiveness is represented by the smallest shaded area on the graph, hope is not lost. They have some options to increase their level of effectiveness.

The first option is to, perhaps, work diligently to increase the drive for better results. The goal would be to raise that six to a nine.

If this person worked individually and drove others with great intensity to achieve this, his Effectiveness Quotient would have increased by only 50 percent. And there would probably be "dead bodies" lying around.

There'd be better results but at the expense of the majority of this person's relationships—both professional and personal.

The second option is for this person to strive to increase his people skills and level of relationships. You might be thinking, "Bobby, if I take time to focus on developing people and relationships, won't my results suffer?"

That's a good question. Again, it is not an either-or situation. Let's look at the second Effectiveness Quotient graph.

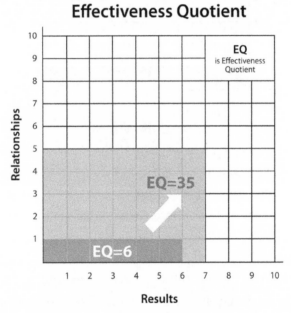

Suppose, through some personal development, this person now raises his relationship skills from one to five. In my experience and observations, the level of the person's results will also increase, possibly from six to seven, with no added intentional effort in that area.

The total Effectiveness Quotient will now be thirty-five. This person will have exponentially increased his original effectiveness of six by 583 percent, simply by focusing on the relationship part.

When you enhance relationships as you drive for results, your effectiveness increases exponentially.

Most people, while intelligent and well-meaning, tend to drive for results.

They tell others the results they want, with little or no input from others. These people don't realize that investing in relationships actually helps achieve significantly better results.

A person with a relationship-oriented style prepares others around them for the twists and turns along the path of life. People who feel valued are much more willing to go the extra mile when those twists and turns happen—and they always happen.

Treat other people like robots, however, and watch production and satisfaction plummet. Instead of taking ownership and trying to solve problems, people, feeling overwhelmed and disregarded, will shift blame and responsibilities to others.

The path of effectiveness includes both relationships *and* results.

Reflect to Connect

1. Is your focus on relationships or results?
2. How would you rate your effectiveness?
3. How can you improve your EQ?

Examples of Prioritizing Content over Process in America

Often today, the focus is about "my rights" (my freedom) to say and do whatever I want to say and do, whenever I want to say and do it, to whom I want to say and do it to, wherever I want to say and do it, and how I want to say and do it—without regard of others' rights. This thinking is the epitome of freedom *from* responsibility.

*A people that values its privileges
above its principles soon loses both.*
–Dwight Eisenhower

The truth is that it is just as important to focus on process (how you say and do it) as it is to focus on content (what you say and do). It is, also, just as important to focus on people (enhance relationships) as it is to focus on things (drive for results). Process and content are equally important, as can be seen in the following examples.

Putting Down Others

Just watch our leaders put other people down while thinking it builds themselves up. Are you a "picker upper" or "putter downer"?

Picker uppers lift others up so they can serve them more. They come "to serve, not be served." Their focus is on *we*.

Putter downers put others down, thinking this will make others serve them more. They expect others to serve them, not the other way around. Their focus is on *me*. They are ladder climbers, not ladder builders.

People may hear words, but they feel your attitude.
–John Maxwell

They call "good, evil and evil, good." Then we wonder why "We the People" are so mixed up. We do not know and behave according to our nation's core values and purpose.

Hurting people hurt people.

In the news media, watch, listen, and read the reporters who, with biased motives, become the story rather than tell the story. They even use false, misleading, or unverified facts in their reporting. Then "We the People" wonder why so many people have become so cynical searching for the truth.

Furthermore, to expediently gain popularity, our country's leaders, as well as leaders in business, education, and religion, can tell a lie often enough so that it seems to be the truth. Then they will follow the lie up by saying, "That is what America is all about," which is another lie. These lies are rooted in selfish motives to gain more power, possessions, and position—in a word, pride.

> *If you tell a big enough lie and tell it frequently enough, it will be believed.*
> **–Adolf Hitler**

Division over Diversity

Think back to the communities of prior generations. Your parents or grandparents may have disagreed with their neighbor regarding politics, but they also shared common bonds of friendship and community. The political discussions at the barbershop were silenced on Friday nights when the whole town came together to root for the home football team.

Now, our political disagreements become shouting matches, with each party thinking about *me* and neither considering *we*. Consequently, we accentuate our differences and overlook opportunities to come together.

At the expense of enhancing relationships where all Americans, everyone, is on the same American Team, "We the People" put people into "silos" or buckets—identity politics.

Therefore, America has become further divided to the point people ask, who is "us" and who is "them"? When this occurs, people discriminate in favor of their in-group members. As group-based policies continue to multiply, affirmative action demands that people be treated as groups, and it is likely to end with more self-segregation and fewer cross-diversity friendships. This will build stronger feelings of alienation.

When we face a common threat or challenge, we are inclined to work together, striving for the team win. However, if I see everyone as a competitor, I'm okay with your loss because it means my win.

There is in fact a manly and legitimate passion for equality that spurs all men to wish to be strong and esteemed. This passion tends to elevate the lesser to the rank of the greater. But one also finds in the human heart a depraved taste for equality, which impels the weak to want to bring the strong down to their level, and which reduces men to preferring equality in servitude to inequality in freedom.

–Alexis de Tocqueville

Those in higher education have pushed for greater diversity under the banner of education while concealing their underlying political agenda. This politically motivated diversity has created dissension on college campuses, with students segregated into special interests (me) and unwilling to consider the perspectives of others (we).

Mass media and social media have given us a "firehose" of information of diversity bias, and they tend to go into overdrive to share an extreme version of any story to keep their audience engaged. Things aren't merely interesting; they're extremely dramatic.

Social media's algorithms and artificial intelligence tend to lump us into buckets and feed us information that more or less conforms to what we have previously showed an interest in—further dividing and polarizing us. As a result, when inaccurate information infects one of these diverse echo chambers with millions of people, there are few checks on its spread.

The solution is to return America back to the bedrock that has made us unique in the history of the world. It would return us to America's core values, freedom and responsibility, and America's purpose, religious freedom. Thus, we would see ourselves as Americans, with equal opportunity for all, regardless of how diverse we are.

Radical Methodology

Have you noticed a pattern developing over the last several years in the behavior of our national, state, and local political leaders? This same approach is also echoed by news media and community and organizational activists. Their behavior stems from a methodology with the following characteristics.

- The main objective is to obtain power.
- They choose an "enemy" to target and destroy.
- The "means" (what you say and do, and how you say and do it), even if you ridicule, lie, cheat, and steal, does not matter as long as you achieve the "end" result.
- Instead of encouraging the steady growth and improvement of our great nation, they only compare America to a utopic picture of perfection. Institutions are to be destroyed to achieve this perfection.

Power tends to corrupt, and absolute power corrupts absolutely.
–Lord Acton

Saul Alinsky's most famous book about this methodology, *Rules for Radicals: A Pragmatic Primer for Realistic Radicals* (1971), includes a dedication to "the first radical known to man who rebelled against the establishment and did it so effectively that he at least won his own kingdom—Lucifer."

In contrast to Alinsky's approach, Ronald Reagan declared,

Without God there is no virtue, because there's no prompting of the conscience. Without God, we're mired in the material, that flat world that tells us only what the senses perceive. Without God, there is a coarsening of the society. And without God, democracy will not and cannot long endure.

Alinsky's methodology is deeply rooted and expansive in our political process. Would you be surprised to know that a recent past US President taught this methodology to activists for about two years? Would you be surprised to know that a recent presidential party nominee worked as an intern under Alinsky and wrote a ninety-two-page college thesis on this methodology?

Failing to adopt the principle of process and content represents another crack in the foundation of our divided nation.

Since the core values of the United States of America are freedom *and* responsibility, freedom is our *what* (what are my rights)—a thing. It is about *me*—my drive for results. Responsibility is our *how* (how we behave)—about people. It is about *we*—to enhance relationships.

What we say and do (content) always precedes *how* we say and do it (process). Until we know and understand our "what" (freedom), we cannot demonstrate our "how" (responsibility). So, to be most effective, we need both process and content—freedom and responsibility—which we'll talk more about in the next chapter.

Reflect to Connect

1. Do we truly have freedom when we behave irresponsibly by ignoring process and relationships?
2. Do you see that you gain freedom when you behave responsibly?
3. In today's news, can you find examples of irresponsible, me-centric behavior?

CHAPTER ELEVEN:

A Two-Prong Strategy for Success

Putting Process and Content into Practice

Success is about yourself. Significance is about others.
Once you've tasted significance, success will never satisfy!
—John Maxwell

I've found that most folks tend to live their lives focused on things, not people. You know what I'm talking about. In our personal life, it includes smartphones, money, automobiles, clothes, and houses; in business, it includes phone calls to make, materials or equipment to purchase, reports to complete, and financial statements to review.

The more these things stack up, the more quickly we want to handle them so we can get on with other things. These are the *what* items that we habitually focus on while often not slowing down long enough to adequately think about the *how*, the process.

So why don't people pursue process as well as content? Here is the problem: in our busy environment, we tend toward expediency. We pursue individual and work goals that are self-focused. We're focused on *me*.

It is very easy to slip into expediently fulfilling *our own* narrow needs without giving sufficient attention to the *needs of others* and how we might better fulfill the overall needs of other people. We ignore the needs of *we*.

For example, it's natural for salespeople to want to increase their sales. Similarly, manufacturing people want to reduce their costs, minimize the production of imperfect products, and eliminate lost-time accidents. Administrative people, such as accountants and Human Resource staff members, want to produce accurate records and minimize employee turnover, respectively.

In each of these pursuits, our focus tends to be on quickly and successfully handling the content targets of our own specialties without giving sufficient attention to *how* our challenges and opportunities fit into the overall organization's goals. Self-serving efforts to save a dollar might have two dollars' worth of negative consequences on another department.

In other words, practicing, "Ready, aim, fire!" should take precedence over, "Fire, ready, aim!" Expedient, work-focused achievements can give quick results, but they may also produce a feeling of personal satisfaction at the expense of big-picture team effectiveness.

The following are some other reasons why people don't pursue process as well as content:

- A person who is bright, knowledgeable, dedicated, decisive, and dependable may also be impatient and intolerant when dealing with others.
- A person may think he has to give up results (content) to enhance relationships (process). As we've seen, this way of thinking is not correct. It is *not* either-or. The most effective approach embraces both process *and* content.
- Some also think that process is not always the right approach. There may be times a process-oriented strategy isn't best (e.g.,

when a leader commands everyone to leave the building because of a fire), but it's generally the most powerful approach a person can take when driving for results.

There are many concerns that get in the way of people fully applying this principle of process and content. Anyone can, however, make conscious decisions to learn and leverage this powerful principle.

Observation: The principles of process and content were on display at the birth of America. Consider the colonists' frustration at the dominating leadership of the English monarchy. Those in power focused on results (content–me) and ignored the relationships (process–we) of those who risked their lives to journey to America. This lopsided approach led to the unbearable situation that resulted in the American Revolution.

So, how can we adopt this approach of process and content? It all starts by raising our awareness. Instead of first blaming someone else for strained relationships or substandard results, we should take a look in the mirror. We should ask ourselves, how well do I

- Listen to others?
- Communicate with others?
- Understand, cooperate, and collaborate with others?
- Praise and appreciate those around me?

Always remember that the most important things in the world aren't *things*. They're people and relationships. The Founding Fathers understood this. Hopefully each of us will, too.

Reflect to Connect

1. Has a primarily results-focused approach trapped you into strained relationships and disappointing results?
2. Based on your calendar and daily agenda, which do you value more, people or things?

The Paradox of Process

Most people sincerely believe it takes too much time and effort to adopt a more process-oriented lifestyle.

This approach is too difficult to understand, they think, and they say to themselves, "I've got things to do, and other people have things to do as well."

This type of thinking results in millions of people throughout America who are

- Unaware of their personal core values and purpose.
- Unaware of what their personal goals are.
- Unclear about what is expected of themselves.
- Uncertain about others' perceptions as to how well they say and do things.
- Unsure about how they might be more effective or efficient in life.
- Uninformed about what degrees of freedom and responsibility they must have to seek "Life, Liberty, and the pursuit of Happiness."

Consequently, many potentially wonderful people become frustrated with our country's leadership. That's the bad news.

The good news is that these challenges represent unequaled opportunities for improved understanding. And the more open the communication atmosphere is for conversations vertically and horizontally, the greater the opportunity for people to address decisions in principled (instead of expedient) ways.

The paradox of process is this: what we bemoan as "extra and unnecessary" time invested in people actually opens the door to achieving the results we have pursued for so long.

We need to focus on both process and content—not simply one or the other. If we can get past the scarcity mindset that leads to expedient behaviors, we can enjoy the abundance that results from selflessness—when you go about "to serve, not be served."

Every process-oriented person can achieve positive outcomes and results as they tap the power of process *and* content.

Here's a list of benefits:

- People feel good about themselves because they have a sense of achievement and enjoy receiving recognition for whatever has been achieved.

- People really appreciate being appreciated. They enjoy being respected as useful, as one whose opinions are important. They are excited to be respected as valuable "thinkers" as well as "doers."

- Other people you interact with appreciate being dealt with respectfully and are delighted you enthusiastically chose to serve them.

- Other people become truly inspired and enhance their chances for success.

- Morale and teamwork increase, which leads to improved performance and optimum results. Your impact is multiplied, not just added.

- It's no wonder such folks become cheerleaders of your approach.

- People who are invited to engage in the communication process are likely to gain a better understanding of the results they are expected to achieve and why it is important to achieve these results.
- People who are part of the process feel their opinion is valued and are more likely to be committed to working within the team to achieve the results.
- People feel they are working for a higher purpose.

As all of these factors come together, people are highly motivated and experience high-performance results.

When people engage others with process and content, they become enthusiastic about the conversation, show initiative, and loyally devote themselves to furthering everyone's reputation and interest.

This extra level of effort and contribution is called "discretionary effort." It is giving over and above what is required. It's like finding the goose that lays the golden eggs.

By adopting the principles of process *and* content, you will have to spend some extra time and effort, but the results will far exceed the additional investment in yourself and others.

Reflect to Connect

1. Why do you think we tend to overestimate the value of the content (the results we want to accomplish) and underestimate the value of the process (to enhance relationships)?
2. What steps can you take today to start earning the enthusiasm, initiative, and devotion of others?
3. Can you identify one way that you can tap the power of process today?

Leverage Your Effectiveness

In the previous chapter, I talked about the Effectiveness Quotient, where the more you focus on relationships, the better your results.

Over the years, I have also observed that people are generally more focused on results than relationships.

As we pursue both process and content, most of us will need to focus on how we interact with people to set and pursue our goals.

For example, at work, focusing on good process as well as content is a matter of leadership style. For example, authoritarian types of people are task-oriented and prone to rely on their position of authority with a desire to direct others. They tend to focus only on the results and what they want to say and do most *efficiently*.

They leave little or no room for others to contribute to the discussion or decision-making process. In the extreme, these people expect others to just follow orders without ever challenging them or questioning their statement or command.

By contrast, process-oriented people create an open atmosphere. They solicit input from others at the very beginning of the discussion or decision-making process because they want the benefit of others' thoughts before making a decision. They tend to understand they need both relationships and results to be most *effective*.

I have learned that focusing on good process is the best way to obtain the desired result, and I have grown to absolutely trust a "process-oriented" approach to life. Why? Because when I trust good process, I always get good results.

Therefore, when you understand and implement the two-pronged approach of process *and* content, you'll multiply your impact with others.

The same principle applies to our personal relationships as well. The other day, I spoke with a good friend who grew up in a very wealthy family, one so affluent that the children were driven to school by a chauffeur. This friend said, "If your dad gave you everything but never had time for you, the things would not mean anything because there would be no relationship attached to the things." What a powerful statement.

In this scenario, do you see how my friend's dad was focused on the things (the content) but not the relationship? I can almost hear him say, "I give my kids everything they could ever want."

Yet the kids felt unloved and unappreciated and were desperate to spend quality time with their father. In the father's mind, the gifts proved that he loved his kids. But in his kids' minds, the effectiveness of his gifts was dependent on the depth of the relationship he had with them.

This represents the process part of the story, which speaks to the power of emotionally connecting with people to form strong relationships.

To be good parents, leaders, employees, and spouses, we need both process *and* content. We need both the "how" and the "what," not one or the other. How we say and do things matters.

Yes, it's awfully easy in the short run to make quick decisions on our own and to be curt and directive in giving instructions or making statements. (Just think about how much easier it might sometimes seem to pick up your child's room rather than to patiently give little Emily repeated instructions and direction.) However, it takes incredibly little additional time and effort to allow others

- To contribute their thoughts on pending decisions.
- To encourage involvement.
- To ask for commitments instead of demanding them.
- To be constructive and supportive when seeking improvement.
- To be able to disagree without being disagreeable.
- To capitalize on the creative ideas and support of all those who can contribute to making good things happen.

What does it take to improve the way one interacts with others? An understanding of people's desires and needs, coupled with nominal investments of time and effort to tap the power of process, will yield wonderful long-term returns.

Reflect to Connect

1. Are you more authoritarian or more process oriented?
2. What steps should you take to multiply your impact with others?
3. If you are a parent, how are you prioritizing relationships and results with your children?

Process-Oriented Communication

Just as a process-oriented approach can radically boost your results and cohesion among your relationships, this same approach can work wonders in your communication skills.

Anyone can improve his or her influence and communication by understanding the following truth:

How something is said is often more important than what is said.

How do you communicate and interact with people on a day-to-day basis? If you haven't given that much thought, I challenge you to pay close attention to your conversations today.

How you say something can significantly impact what the recipient of the message *feels* is being conveyed. Our physical actions and tone of voice can reinforce or contradict the message in the words we are saying.

When the way that something is said (process) conveys a different meaning than the actual words (content), the interpretation triggered by the process will prevail.

For example, when two old friends meet after many years of separation, one might say, "George, you old dog!"

The words themselves may be negative, but if they are spoken with a ring in the voice and a smile, George will have no doubt that his friend is delighted to see him.

The way things are said can also override the meaning of the words themselves with sarcastic comments. A negative pitch of voice has the power to dominate positive words.

If the way we say something is out of alignment with what we are saying, the way we say it will always dominate the communication.

Your English teacher always said that punctuation was important. And, as with punctuation, just changing what you say by using a pause (an auditory comma) can make a big difference in meaning, too. For example:

- Let's eat grandma!
- Let's eat, grandma!

See the difference? One sentence is quite disturbing, while the other is a simple call to dinner.

But what about those who argue that content is all-important? "I may not have time to worry about *how* I say something," the content-oriented person points out. "It's much faster to be brief and concise and get on with the work and life at hand. What's right is right, and that's all that should matter!"

With that point, I respectfully disagree. Yes, there are times when you can't worry about how you say something (although it might be better if you did). But the majority of your communications should be well-thought-out, and, whenever possible, you should consider how your message will be received.

When trying to build and strengthen interpersonal relationships, an attitude of "what's right is right" can be absolutely wrong. We may make no better investment than the small amount of time and effort required to improve the way things are said and done.

Certainly, some conditions require quick, authoritarian action. However, during noncritical periods—which comprise the majority of the time in our daily life—it is best to interact in a process-oriented way.

Reflect to Connect

1. If the content is what is said and the process is how we say it, where do you see the most opportunity for improvement in your life?

2. Have you ever had how you communicated (process) override what you were saying (content)?

3. How can you apply the powerful principle of process and content?

PART THREE

Where Do We Go from Here?

CHAPTER TWELVE:

The Challenge and the Hope

Only a virtuous people are capable of freedom.
As nations become more corrupt and vicious,
they have more need of masters.

—Benjamin Franklin

James Madison knew that he was not an impressive figure. Sick often throughout his childhood, he had grown up short and thin, and his speaking voice was quiet. He tended to mumble.

But his mind was sharper than most men's minds. And now he turned his mind to a particular problem: making sure that the infant America survived.

Madison had never seen battle. He spent the war in the halls of legislatures in Virginia and in New York, where the Congress of the Confederation met. This body, established by the Articles of Confederation that bound thirteen states together just firmly enough to prosecute the Revolution, was a stop-gap measure.

So he lobbied the most important men of his day—some fellow delegates to the Congress, some not—to create a conference to replace the Articles of Confederation with something that could last. The result was the Constitutional Convention held in Philadelphia over the long, hot summer of 1787.

Madison left little to chance regarding that meeting. He borrowed two thousand books from Thomas Jefferson on constitutional law and history, and he used those volumes and his own genius to write the Virginia Plan, a rough draft of a new Constitution, before he traveled to Pennsylvania.

In a wisely strategic move, he stood aside and let Edmund Randolph, his state's governor and a more powerful man, present the Virginia Plan to the Convention. And Madison not only recorded the debates of that convention for posterity, but he also spoke over two hundred times.

In the streets outside Independence Hall, as the story is often told, Philadelphians waited to see what kind of government Madison and the other delegates had decided on.

"What have we got?" a woman asked Ben Franklin.

"A Republic, if you can keep it," he replied.[14]

When the Constitutional Convention ended in September, Madison could have gone home to his huge plantation, bitten his nails, and waited anxiously to see whether the states would ratify the Constitution that the Convention had created.

But he would not leave so much to chance. Instead, he joined forces with future Secretary of the Treasury Alexander Hamilton and future Supreme Court Justice John Jay to write the most clear and salient explanation of what government ought to be and to do that the world had ever seen.

These powerful men could have published a book available only to those rich enough to invest in such a treasure. But they chose to publish all their essays one at a time in New York newspapers, available to anyone who could spare the penny to buy them or who could sit in a tavern long enough to hear one read.

They put their lofty thoughts in plain language and delivered them into the hands of the masses, sparking a love for the Constitution in the hearts of Americans that lasts to this day.

Madison knew that he had something important and lasting to give to his fledgling country, a common thread that would bind her people together and ensure her survival.

And because he valued the people around him, set aside his own pride, worked tirelessly with no recompense, and trusted reason instead of anger to fight his battles, James Madison, our fourth president, is known as the Father of the Constitution. He was also primarily responsible for the Bill of Rights.[15]

We have staked the whole future of our new nation, not upon the power of government; far from it. We have staked the future of all our political constitutions upon the capacity of each of ourselves to govern ourselves according to the moral principles of the Ten Commandments of God.

–James Madison

The Challenge

In the four cultural problems mentioned earlier in the book—Principle vs. Expediency, Abundance vs. Scarcity Mindset, Symptoms vs. Root Cause, and Process and Content—one common thread hints at a common solution. The answer is found in *leadership*.

Each of these problems needs leaders, like James Madison, who are principled and responsible in what they say and do. Every significant change in history has been birthed by the vision, passion, and leadership of courageous men and women. And the most effective way to inspire and stimulate change is at the top, through a leader of leaders.

That is why I believe that the best place to start a rebirth is with the president of the United States of America.

Everything rises and falls on leadership.
–John Maxwell

The leader of our country has a unique opportunity to start the journey to restore our country's core values (who we are) and purpose (why we exist).

Imagine our president declaring he or she will live out the core values of freedom and responsibility within their administration and require the same commitment in the federal agencies that report to them.

Can you envision Congress and the Supreme Court aligning with the president's leadership and also choosing to live out our nation's core values and purpose as our moral compass?

Consider the impact as business leaders, educators, clergy, and families adopt a principled approach that acknowledges the importance of both freedom *and* responsibility.

Reflect to Connect

1. Can you envision the impact of a president who understands the purpose of America and embodies the core values of freedom and responsibility?
2. What changes would we see if the leaders of business, education, and religion understood America's purpose and exemplified her core values?

Our Responsibility

Have you ever noticed that the Constitution of the United States of America has a Bill of Rights, but it does not have a Bill of Responsibilities? The reason for this is simple: when our country was founded, people generally knew how to be responsible and self-governing.

How? Our country came into existence for religious freedom (our purpose). And, as we mentioned in Part One, since the only textbook that generally existed was the Bible, families and schools used it to teach the standards of responsibility. That was how people knew how to behave in a responsible and principled way.

Remember the foundational truth from the Bible: each person is responsible for their actions. More specifically, it says we are each responsible for our own wrongdoing, or sin, but faith opens the door for us to receive freedom from the burden of our wrongdoing.

At this point, some people will say, in an expedient way, "We are an advanced society and a prosperous country. We can handle these problems that you have laid out. And you have also gone too far by asking us to turn back our clocks to embrace the principled ideals of our past." We are, indeed, free to make our decisions, but the outcomes and consequences that we experience are inexorably linked to those decisions.

The truth is "We the People of the United States of America" are going at warp speed back to Sodom and Gomorrah. Unless we change the trajectory of our nation we will soon see the following:

- Trading for sex slaves and adults having sex with children—which today is a horrible thought—will become acceptable in our culture.

- People will justify immoral and illegal conduct by citing the disadvantaged childhood of the criminal. No one will speak up for the true victim, but people will defend the activity of the offender and claim that *he* is the victim.

- Business leaders will push for a hands-off approach, a "complete" openness of the internet to consumers, for economic growth and profits for the shareholders and themselves. Such profits will accrue without a sense of responsibility for such freedom and, consequently, will usher in norms that are now considered unconscionable, like sex trafficking and abuse. (It is interesting that many businesses have taken responsibility for what employees' eyes can see and what their ears can hear when using their own networks to get on the internet.)

Freedom requires virtue, which requires faith, which requires freedom, which in turn requires virtue, which requires faith, which requires freedom.
–Os Guinness

It is also interesting that when people, in a principled way, show respect, dignity, and love toward others, we do not need laws and regulations to tell us to do so.

Remember, trust is the foundation of leadership.

People will follow a worthy leader before they will follow a worthy cause.

A worthy leader behaves in a responsible and principled way. However, the leader must first believe in the people before the people believe in the leader.

Some might argue that binding our freedoms with responsibility will limit our freedoms. But don't miss the wisdom of The Freedom Paradox:

The more we behave irresponsibly, the more freedoms we lose. The more we embrace responsibility, the greater freedoms we enjoy.

Individual rights assume individual responsibility. So . . .

Let us do what is responsible instead of what is permissible.

Let's leverage our individual rights for the benefit of others and, thereby, prevent our freedom from devouring itself and us.

Reflect to Connect

1. Do you see signs of civil unrest in your community?
2. How can you leverage your rights for the benefit of others? (i.e., How can you think *we* instead of *me*)?

Consider these examples of how acting responsibly can impact our situation:

- If I drive responsibly, I no longer read or send text messages while I'm driving, even though I have the freedom to do so. This results in fewer accidents and reduces the chance of bodily injury or death to myself or another person. In addition, it reduces the likelihood of automobile and property damage.
- If, as an able-bodied person, I find gainful employment, I responsibly meet the needs of my family and provide for those I love. This builds my self-esteem, creates meaningful opportunities for advancement, and decreases the role of government to provide for my long-term needs.

This is why I feel compelled to express my thoughts because I'm reminded of the story titled "Whose Job Is It, Anyway?"

This is a story about four people named Everybody, Somebody, Anybody, and Nobody. There was an important job to be done, and Everybody was sure that Somebody would do it. Anybody could have done it, but Nobody did it. Somebody got angry about that because it was Everybody's job. Everybody thought Anybody could do it, but Nobody realized that Everybody wouldn't do it. It ended up that

Everybody blamed Somebody when Nobody did what
Anybody could have done.
—Author Unknown

The message is clear: no one took responsibility, so nothing got accomplished.

America, let's stop playing the game of life not to lose. Let's play the game to win and win big.

Let's avoid allowing America to become Everybody, Somebody, Anybody, and Nobody, and may each one of us commit to becoming the kind of person who takes responsibility for our own lives.

Let's not allow Anybody (or Everybody, Somebody, or Nobody) to stop us from doing what "We the People" need to do to create the kind of modeled, moral life we can be proud of.

I also feel compelled to express my thoughts because I'm reminded of Martin Niemoller, who was an outspoken public foe of Adolf Hitler following the Nazis' rise to power and the subsequent purging of their chosen groups. Consider Niemoller's remarks:

In Germany they came first for the Communists, and I didn't speak up—because I wasn't a Communist.

Then they came for the Jews, and I didn't speak up—because I wasn't a Jew.

Then they came for the trade unionists, and I didn't speak up—because I wasn't a trade unionist.

Then they came for the Catholics, and I didn't speak up—because I was a Protestant.

Then they came for me—and by that time no one was left to speak up.

America, I think I understand where you are, who you are, and why you exist. We can rebuild your foundation from the top-down and from the bottom-up. Remember, leadership is a dialogue, not a *monologue*.

Our president can be the catalyst to engage "We the People" for this significant change by centering his or her administration and leadership around the core values of freedom and responsibility and our purpose of religious freedom.

In turn, we can spark change in our own areas of influence. How can you model principled living and leadership to your family, local schools, and place of worship? How can you exemplify our nation's core values of freedom *and* responsibility?

What principles would you suggest we include in a Bill of Responsibilities? You can share your ideas at www.BobbyAlbert.com/ BillOfResponsibilities.

Reflect to Connect

1. Do you see people pursuing their freedom but ignoring their corresponding responsibilities?
2. How can you participate in the "freedom dialogue" and help start rebuilding the foundation of America?
3. What would you suggest be added to a Bill of Responsibilities?

The Hope

George Washington stood on the balcony of the Federal Hall in New York, looking down at the enthusiastic crowd of newly minted Americans. They had done it—all of them together.

They had won a dangerous and exhausting war, crafted an ingenious political machine, and set it in motion with their unanimous election of him as president.

He took his oath of office and gravely acknowledged the cheers and tossed hats that celebrated him. The people below him believed he was set apart from the political divisions that tore them and the regional differences that troubled them.

Washington belonged to all of them. Because of their faith and their trust, he was the only man who could serve at this moment in the office he had just sworn to uphold. He was celebrated as "the man who unites all hearts."

Gravely, Washington walked inside to the assembled Congress, which reminded him so strongly of the men who had come together under his leadership nearly two years before to craft the Constitution. Now these men would use it.

They would soon find out whether the machine could run this nation. He had carefully considered what he should say to them at this moment, whittling his original seventy-three-page epic into a manageable twenty-minute address.

Now the moment had come. And he found that the most salient mission he could urge on them was the one they had already undertaken: to maintain the healthy tension between freedom and responsibility.

These national leaders before him must take to heart and take back to their states the message that liberty and virtue deserved equal esteem. This nation they had brought to life must live in the hearts of each citizen as that citizen embraced virtue as a guarantee of his own liberty. Washington impressed upon his hearers a sense of personal responsibility:

The foundations of our national policy will be laid in the pure and immutable principles of private morality; and the pre-eminence of free government, be exemplified by all the attributes which can win the affections of its citizens, and command the respect of the world . . . There exists in the economy and course of nature, an indissoluble union between virtue and happiness; between duty and advantage, between genuine maxims of an honest and magnanimous policy, and the solid rewards of public prosperity and felicity.

Since we ought to be no less persuaded that the propitious smiles of heaven can never be expected on a nation that disregards the eternal rules of order and right, which heaven itself has ordained.

And since the preservation of the sacred fire of liberty, and the destiny of the republican model of government, are justly considered as deeply, perhaps as finally staked on the experiment entrusted to the hands of the American people.

This government, no matter the skill or devotion or strength of its leader, could not survive without the corresponding greatness of its people.

Washington ceased speaking and looked solemnly at the men assembled before him, willing them to impress this message on their hearts and minds. He might have very well been thinking, *Be good men, for you cannot be free if you will not be good.*[16]

The kind of freedom Washington referred to was more than just political freedom—it was also an inner freedom.

Can you just imagine what America would look like if every citizen experienced this kind of inward freedom and outward freedom? If every citizen was physically free to pursue life, liberty, and happiness and was free from anxiety or fear?

Perhaps it would be as author Bill Tinsley envisions:

There would be no more crime. Theft, violence and murder would end. Prisons would empty. Neighbor would no longer sue neighbor. Court dockets would clear.

Employers would forego extravagant profits in order to pay higher wages to their workers. No child would go to bed hungry or unsheltered. Those who possess the food and resources of the world would share with those who have none.

Corruption, graft and greed would disappear. Wars would cease. Politicians would serve the best interest of others with honesty and integrity. Fairness, kindness, forgiveness and generosity would prevail.

Husbands would love their wives seeking what is best for them and striving to please them. Wives would love and respect their husbands, building them up and encouraging them. Children would honor their parents and obey them, trusting them in the knowledge that they want what is best for them.

Racial, cultural and sexual prejudices would vanish. Discrimination would disappear. Every human being would treat every other human being with respect. The strong would help the weak.[17]

Would you like to know true freedom from the inside out? It takes more than just knowing our country's core values and purpose. It will require a change of the condition of your heart, but there is only One who can change the condition of your heart. It is not what you do but who you trust to receive this true freedom.

If you are seeking this *true* freedom, please go to PeacewithGod.net or begin an electronic chat at chataboutjesus.com.

Reflect to Connect

1. Would you like to experience the America described by Bill Tinsley above?
2. Do you agree with the statement, "Lasting change happens from the inside out"? Why?

CONCLUSION:

Our Freedom *and* Responsibility

The more freedom we enjoy, the greater the responsibility we bear, toward others as well as ourselves.

—Oscar Arias

I've been researching for this book and crafting its text for years. From the findings of Jim Collins in *Built to Last* and my many years in business, I realized the importance of founders—of an organization or a nation. So, I dug into the writings of our Founding Fathers and the documents that declared our independence and formed our nation. Those findings, coupled with my observations of our current cultural trends, formed the basis for this book.

In November 1994, former British Prime Minister Margaret Thatcher stepped to the podium and delivered a speech entitled "The Moral Foundations of the American Founding" to an audience of twenty-five hundred students, faculty, and guests of Hillsdale College, Hillsdale, Michigan.

When I first read this speech, I was speechless. So many of her observations and assertions aligned with my own views.

As I thought about the conclusion for this present book, I realized that, in many ways, Lady Thatcher had written a far better conclusion than I could ever write. What follows are excerpts from that 1994 speech. (The complete account of the speech can be found at https://imprimis. hillsdale.edu/the-moral-foundations-of-society/.)[18]

Ironically, the longest serving British prime minister of the 20th century described and commended the very nation birthed from those who were discontented with her own:

History has taught us that freedom cannot long survive unless it is based on moral foundations. The American founding bears ample witness to this fact. America has become the most powerful nation in history, yet she uses her power not for territorial expansion but to perpetuate freedom and justice throughout the world.

For over two centuries, Americans have held fast to their belief in freedom for all men—a belief that springs from their spiritual heritage. John Adams, second president of the United States, wrote in 1789,

"Our Constitution was designed only for a moral and religious people. It is wholly inadequate for the government of any other."

John Winthrop, who led the Great Migration to America in the early 17th century, told the members of his company that they must rise to their responsibilities and learn to live as God intended men should live: in charity, love, and cooperation with one another.

[The colonists] did not feel they had the liberty to worship freely and, therefore, to live freely, at home. With enormous

courage, the first American colonists set out on a perilous journey to an unknown land—without government subsidies and not in order to amass fortunes but to fulfill their faith.

Christianity is based on the belief in a single God as evolved from Judaism. Most important of all, the faith of America's founders affirmed the sanctity of each individual. Every human life—man or woman, child or adult, commoner or aristocrat, rich or poor—was equal in the eyes of the Lord. It also affirmed the responsibility of each individual.

This was not a faith that allowed people to do whatever they wished, regardless of the consequences.

Thus, they shared a deep sense of obligation to one another. And, as the years passed, they not only formed strong communities but devised laws that would protect individual freedom— laws that would eventually be enshrined in the Declaration of Independence and the US Constitution.

So long as freedom, that is, freedom with responsibility, is grounded in morality and religion, it will last far longer than the kind that is grounded only in abstract, philosophical notions. It is hard not to believe that these gifts were given by a divine Creator, who alone can unlock the secrets of existence.

The most important problems we have to tackle today are problems, ultimately, having to do with the moral foundations of society. There are people who eagerly accept their own freedom but do not respect the freedom of others—they want freedom from responsibility. But if they accept freedom for themselves, they must respect the freedom of others. If they expect to go about their business unhindered and to be protected from violence, they must not hinder the business of or do violence to others.

But it would be a grave mistake to think that freedom requires nothing of us. Each of us has to earn freedom anew in order to possess it.

It is a humbling experience to have one of the great leaders of our lifetime echo many of the same observations and conclusions as your own. I believe such alignment of thought and reason affirm the honest assessment of the founding and foundation of this great country, and I hope it has helped you understand what makes this nation great.

Most important, I hope you have moved from frustrated to equipped, from disillusioned to encouraged. It will take a top-down *and* bottom-up approach to once again align America with her purpose of religious freedom and personify her core values of freedom and responsibility. Once informed and inspired, I believe that you and I, together with the leaders of this country, offer the best hope to reunite our divided nation.

America! America! God shed his grace on thee and crown thy good with brotherhood from sea to shining sea!
–America the Beautiful

ACKNOWLEDGMENTS

I would like to thank all of the people who, over many years, made me look better than I really am.

To Jim Lundy, who was my long-term executive mentor and friend and who took a young, ambitious leader and chipped away the imperfections to make me better.

To Brady Beshear, our chief operating officer for my new company, Values-Driven Leadership, who speaks truth to me when I need it and has taken my raw writings and made this manuscript look really good.

To Dr. Glenn Beck, DDS, who helped research stories and quotes and who's been a rock-solid, fun, and good friend for fifty years.

To Amanda Rooker, the developmental writer who shaped this manuscript into a better representation of my intended message.

To Sharilyn Grayson, who researched quotes and wrote compelling stories for this manuscript.

To the folks at Morgan James Publishing, especially David Hancock and my good friend Karen Anderson.

ABOUT THE AUTHOR

Entrepreneur, CEO, and leadership expert, Bobby Albert is the distinguished author of *Principled Profits* and *True North Business*. Bobby has made a lifelong study of leadership and workplace culture and their impact on growth and prosperity.

Bobby led the Albert Companies to unprecedented growth—and he did so during one of the most challenging economic periods of our lifetime. Using a values-driven approach, Bobby created a unique workplace culture. The Best 100 Companies to Work for in Texas awarded their coveted designation to the Albert team for the first two years they applied for consideration.

A life-long entrepreneur, Bobby has started twelve different businesses and acquired nine others. His approach to business has been to value people, seek wisdom, embrace humility, and never stop learning.

He is currently president of Values-Driven Leadership, LLC. His passion is to help other leaders build inspiring workplace cultures through values-driven leadership. Bobby writes, speaks, and consults with key leaders to share the principles and practices that he used to grow his company from five employees to an organization of more than 150 team members.

A cycling enthusiast, Bobby has logged almost 100,000 miles on his road bike. He and his wife, Susan, live in north Texas and have three married sons and eight grandchildren.

ENDNOTES

1 "Satisfaction with the United States," Gallup, https://news.gallup.com/poll/1669/general-mood-country.aspx.

2 Thanks to Sharilyn Grayson who compiled this story from the following sources: Time Magazine, *The Making of America: Life, Liberty, and the Pursuit of a Nation* (Time Books, 2005), 12–13; Arthur M. Schlesinger, Jr., *The Cycles of American History* (Houghton Mifflin Company, 1986), 221, 242; Wikipedia contributors, "E pluribus unum," *Wikipedia, The Free Encyclopedia*, https://en.wikipedia.org/w/index.php?title=E_pluribus_unum&oldid=911707704 (accessed September 9, 2019).

3 Grover Furr, "Did George Washington Turn Down an Offer to Be a King? The Story behind the Myth," March 2007, https://msuweb.montclair.edu/~furrg/gbi/docs/kingmyth.html.

4 Nathaniel Philbrick, *Mayflower: A Story of Courage, Community, and War* (Penguin, 2007), 4.

5 Sydney Swift, "James Madison: Mastermind of Religious Freedom," First Liberty, June 14, 2019, https://firstliberty.org/news/james-madison-mastermind-of-religious-freedom/.

6   Po Bronson and Ashley Merryman, "The Creativity Crisis," *Newsweek*, July 10, 2010, https://www.newsweek.com/creativity-crisis-74665.

7   Thanks to Sharilyn Grayson who compiled this story from the following sources: Time Magazine, *The Making of America: Life, Liberty, and the Pursuit of a Nation* (Time Books, 2005), 38–39; Kenneth C. Davis, *America's Hidden History: Untold Tales of the First Pilgrims, Fighting Women, and Forgotten Founders Who Shaped a Nation* (HarperCollins, 2008), 81–118.

8   Thanks to Sharilyn Grayson who compiled this story from the following sources: Time Magazine, *The Making of America: Life, Liberty, and the Pursuit of a Nation* (Time Books, 2005), 44; Kenneth C. Davis, *America's Hidden History: Untold Tales of the First Pilgrims, Fighting Women, and Forgotten Founders Who Shaped a Nation* (HarperCollins, 2008), 119–160.

9   "Guiding Principles," Rotary International, https://www.rotary.org/en/guiding-principles.

10 In large part sourced from Sam Walker, "How to Lead Like George Washington," *Wall Street Journal*, September 22, 2018.

11 Thanks to Sharilyn Grayson who compiled this story from the following sources: Time Magazine, *The Making of America: Life, Liberty, and the Pursuit of a Nation* (Time Books, 2005), 7–23; Kenneth C. Davis, *America's Hidden History: Untold Tales of the First Pilgrims, Fighting Women, and Forgotten Founders Who Shaped a Nation* (HarperCollins, 2008), 119–160.

12 This story about the Army Chaplain Corps is excerpted with permission from Liberty McArtor, "The Chaplain Corps Is as Old as the Revolutionary War—And It's Under Attack," First Liberty, July 26, 2019, https://firstliberty.org/news/the-chaplain-corps/.

13 Daniel Kalder, *The Infernal Library: On Dictators, the Books They Wrote, and Other Catastrophes of Literacy* (Henry Holt and Co., 2018), 20.

14 According to Bartleby.com, this anecdote first appeared in The American Historical Review, vol. 11 (1906), p. 618. See also *Respectfully Quoted: A Dictionary of Quotations Requested from the Congressional Research Service* (Library of Congress, 1989); Bartleby. com, 2003, https://www.bartleby.com/73/1593.html.

15 Thanks to Sharilyn Grayson who compiled this story from the following sources: Wikipedia contributors, "James Madison," *Wikipedia, The Free Encyclopedia,* https://en.wikipedia.org/w/index. php?title=James_Madison&oldid=914156272 (accessed September 9, 2019); Richard Beeman, *Plain, Honest Men: The Making of the American Constitution* (Random House, 2009), 22–40.

16 Thanks to Sharilyn Grayson who compiled this story from the following sources: Richard B. Bernstein with Kym S. Rice, *Are We to Be a Nation? The Making of the Constitution* (Harvard University Press, 1987), 243–246; Time Magazine, *The Making of America: Life, Liberty, and the Pursuit of a Nation* (Time Books, 2005), 74–75; "George Washington's First Inaugural Address, 1789," The Gilder Lehrman Institute of American History AP US History Study Guide, https://ap.gilderlehrman.org/resource/george-washington%27s-first-inaugural-address-1789; Arthur M.

Schlesinger, Jr., *The Cycles of American History* (Houghton Mifflin Company, 1986), 3–22.

17 Bill Tinsley, "Imagine an Amazing 2019," *Ocala StarBanner*, December 26, 2018, https://www.ocala.com/opinion/20181226/bill-tinsley-imagine-amazing-2019.

18 Margaret Thatcher, "The Moral Foundations of Society," *Imprimis*, Volume 24, Number 3 (1995): print and web.

Download All of the Tools and Documents Mentioned in This Book

Consulting

BOBBYALBERT.COM/CONSULTING

Leadership Coaching

DO YOU STRUGGLE TO SCALE YOUR BUSINESS TO THE NEXT LEVEL?

Are you looking for:

- A guide who's been there
- A proven plan to follow
- A listening ear
- Someone to help you with direction and strategy

CONTACT BOBBY TO DISCUSS ONE-ON-ONE AND TEAM COACHING

BOBBYALBERT.COM/CONTACT

Speaking

BOBBYALBERT.COM/SPEAKING

On-site Workshops

TEACH YOUR TEAM, ENGAGE YOUR PEOPLE, INSPIRE LASTING CHANGE

BOBBYALBERT.COM/WORKSHOPS

Other Books from Bobby Albert

In my role with the John Maxwell Company, I've learned and lived leadership with the best of the best. That's why I am so excited about Bobby Albert and this book, *Principled Profits*. This book reveals a proven path to exceptional success. Bobby is truly a leader of leaders, and his book offers you a roadmap to values-driven leadership and success. Outward success is indeed an inside job!"

Mark Cole
CEO, The John Maxwell Company

True North Business is a gift to those who want to lead differently. For those who yearn to create an organization where people are engaged, customers are served, and everyone is working for a bigger purpose, this book shows you how.

Dean Niewolny
CEO, Halftime Institute

AVAILABLE EVERYWHERE
Books Are Sold

Printed in the USA
CPSIA information can be obtained
at www.ICGtesting.com
JSHW022333140824
68134JS00019B/1460